SHOHEI OHTANI

THE AMAZING STORY OF BASEBALL'S TWO-WAY JAPANESE SUPERSTAR

JAY PARIS

FOREWORD BY MARK LANGSTON

SPORTS
PUBLISHING

Sports Publishing books may be purchased in bulk at special discounts for sales promotion, corporate gifts, fund-raising, or educational purposes. Special editions can also be created to specifications. For details, contact the Special Sales Department, Sports Publishing, 307 West 36th Street, 11th Floor, New York, NY 10018 or sportspubbooks@skyhorsepublishing.com.

Sports Publishing® is a registered trademark of Skyhorse Publishing, Inc.®, a Delaware corporation.

Visit our website at www.sportspubbooks.com.

10 9 8 7 6 5 4 3 2 1

Library of Congress Cataloging-in-Publication Data is available on file.

Interior photos by Associated Press, unless otherwise noted
Cover design by Qualcom
Cover photo credit: Getty Images

ISBN: 978-1-68358-483-4
Ebook ISBN: 978-1-68358-303-5

Printed in the United States of America

CONTENTS

Before each Angels game, the song "Send Me An Angel" blasts through the Angel Stadium sound system. I always had two angels at home, and they need to be recognized.

If not for Jack and Jean Paris, my parents, I might not have grown so fond of baseball overall and the local nine in particular. It was because of them, and their trust, that a pint-size kid could cherish the summers of his youth cheering for the California Angels, the Anaheim Angels, and, ultimately, the Los Angeles Angels of Anaheim.

Jack Paris wasn't a sports nut—far from it. His focus was on helping those less fortunate as a dedicated Los Angeles County social worker for more than 30 years.

Jean Paris didn't analyze box scores or batting averages, either. She was busy molding tomorrow's leaders by passionately teaching in nearby Tustin for four decades.

But they appreciated my love of baseball, and they did all they could to see that it flourished. That included letting me ride my Schwinn bike to games, minus a helmet on my head or a cell phone sticking out from my back pocket.

They gave me the OK to arrive at Angels games three hours before the first pitch for batting practice, then hang out for an eternity after the last pitch, just to connect with my favorite Angels.

All of those associated with the Angels were keen in my eyes, but none were cooler than Jack and Jean Paris.

Having Angels in the outfield, and infield, is one thing. But nothing beats sharing a home with them when growing up, and I was blessed to do just that.

Jay Paris

ACKNOWLEDGMENTS

There were few major leaguers who had more attention pointed their way this year than the Angels' Shohei Ohtani. From Los Angeles to New York, from Toyko to Beijing, from Facebook to Twitter, Ohtani's rookie season was written about and debated in a seemingly never-ending conversation.

Shohei Ohtani: The Amazing Story of Baseball's Two-way Japanese Superstar tells his story, on and off the field. But it couldn't have been completed without the tireless efforts by other journalists, and their work was used in researching and writing this book.

That includes Maria Guardado and Avery Yang of mlb.com; Dylan Hernandez, Mike DiGiovanna, Jeff Miller, Bill Shaikin, and Bill Plaschke of the *Los Angeles Times*; Jeff Fletcher of the *Orange County Register*; Scott Miller of Bleacher Report; Bob Nightengale of *USA Today*; Tim Brown of Yahoo Sports; and Jim Allen of Kyodo News in Japan.

FOREWORD

BY MARK LANGSTON

IT WAS A couple of years ago when I first heard the name "Shohei Ohtani" from my mom, of all people. She had seen the *60 Minutes* piece on him on TV and said that this guy Shohei, a Japanese player, was a great story.

Then, for Shohei to later pick the Los Angeles Angels to be his team to begin his career in the majors, out of all the many teams that wanted him, was really fortunate for me.

It gave me the chance to call Angels games with a team that included Mike Trout, the best player in the game of baseball, and Shohei Ohtani, the most exciting player in the game of baseball.

Shohei's rookie season was something we hadn't seen in a century of baseball. And it began with what I think was one of the most anticipated starts to a major-league career.

So many guys come over from Japan with incredible hype. But it's so hard to live up to it because the players are so talented here in the majors.

Then, when Shohei had a disappointing spring training, he didn't have a track record from being in the major leagues. Many guys just flip the switch once the season starts after doing what it takes to get ready in the spring. But we know what they are capable of doing during the season because they have done it before.

But with Shohei, we were just basing what we knew about him off his spring training numbers, and he struggled. There was even talk of him opening the season in Triple A!

In my mind, he had established himself as a pitcher with his stuff, and stuff plays no matter where you play baseball. By stuff, I mean he could throw a baseball 100 miles per hour, and he had that splitter and slider. Those pitches came through loud and clear. He had shown in Japan that he could get people out with his stuff.

Where I thought he would have to prove he could compete was in the batter's box. The adjustments opposing pitchers make are constant, and they are really, really good at it. They will expose any weakness that you have. So, if Shohei was going to struggle, I thought it would be in the batter's box.

But he made the club, and then his first week was just electric. That first hit of his, that first pitching start, those three home runs in his first three home games . . . it was impressive that he made the adjustment so quickly from spring training to the regular season.

That started a season in which there was a buzz whenever Shohei played, both at home and on the road. We would go through towns, and the other teams' radio broadcasters would want to know about him. And fans of those other teams were all wondering about this two-way player that they had heard so much about. They wanted to know what he was about, and they wanted to see him play.

It was fun to see how Shohei was embraced by fans in Southern California. When he pitched, it was an event that was off the charts. Angel Stadium was packed every time he started a game because his stuff was so electric that there was a possibility he could throw a no-hitter every time that he went out there.

Maybe I'm so impressed with Shohei because I played 16 years in the majors and I know how hard it is to be good in even one element of baseball. There is so much preparation involved to be a good hitter. Then there is the intense preparation to be a good pitcher.

For Shohei to excel at both, at a very high level of competition, has blown me away.

When you look at his offensive numbers this year, although with fewer at-bats, they were similar to 2016, his best year in Japan. You see what he is capable of doing at the plate.

Then, in making those 10 starts before he hurt his elbow, he was performing like a top-of-the-rotation guy. I know he won't be able to pitch next year. But the future is so bright for this guy as a pitcher and a hitter.

I say that because of his two-way skills and his incredible mental focus, too.

He drinks, eats, and sleeps baseball. He is focused on becoming an elite player; there is no time to do anything that would take away from that.

You see some players where they say, "Gosh, I'm 35 years old and the end got here quick." That's not going to happen with Shohei because he wants to be a star.

He is driven to excel and be the best that he can be. He doesn't want any excuses, he wants nothing to get in the way of his rest and his preparation.

But he's also a great teammate, and you can tell by the way he's treated. He's still the punk little rookie whom the other players like to tease and have fun with. He gets it, and it's clear he's having fun because he is always smiling.

His teammates love taking him out to dinner, although he gets back early to get his sleep because he is all about focusing on everything to be successful at his job.

I love that about him. He's not taking anything for granted. He knows what he wants to do, and he's going to do it. I'm a big fan of that.

I don't know how he doesn't win the American League Rookie of the Year Award. Considering what he's been able to do on offense, combined with his work on the mound with 50-plus innings with stuff that was electric, I think he should be a slam dunk to win it.

He has done things that are above and beyond what people thought he could do in a rookie season unlike any other in baseball history.

In *Shohei Ohtani: The Amazing Story of Baseball"s Two-Way Japanese Superstar*, Jay Paris, a longtime Southern California sportswriter, takes readers along with Shohei on every step of his exciting rookie season.

Paris also describes how a younger Shohei molded himself into becoming the type of incredible player who has the potential to change the way we think about baseball.

So settle in with these interesting tales to discover more about the sensational Shohei. Or just peel through the pages and relive a season that will be forever cherished not only by myself and Angels fans, but by baseball fans all around the world.

PREFACE

GOING TO ANGELS GAMES WAS HEAVENLY

IN NEARLY EVERY direction someone looked, orange groves filled the view and orange blossoms were the unmistakable fragrance. Orange County, back then, was appropriately named. It was rural and agricultural, with no major professional sports team calling it home.

Then the Angels move to Anaheim in 1966, and it's never really been the same. The Angels brought the big leagues to Orange County, and that started a lifelong love affair with the team for this writer who lived just three miles down the street.

The Big A was just that, and it was so much larger than nearly anything else in the area. For a kid, gazing at that Big A was like peering up at a structure that reminded me of "Jack and the Beanstalk."

Then at night, the halo would blink after the Angels were victorious, and that's how we often learned the game's outcome.

Day games meant riding my bike down to the Big A, a trek that was a straight line to bliss. Of course, it meant getting to the Big A three hours early to watch batting practice and shag balls down the left-field line. Then afterward waiting for the players, getting an autograph or a handshake, and I can't remember many players turning us down.

Among those exiting with the players was Gene Autry, the "Singing Cowboy" and Angels owner. Autry loved youngsters, and he never passed us by—usually with All-Star shortstop Jim Fregosi on his hip—without patting our heads. No one was nicer than Mr. Autry, but I later found out he treated everyone that way.

But back in my Little League days, many players were like Shohei Ohtani. They pitched, they batted, and they had fun. But, as we know, Major League Baseball frowned on players doing both—until Ohtani arrived for his historic rookie season.

Watching Ohtani rekindled a spark in me, as he took me back to when I was kid riding my bike to the Big A. He played the game on his terms, and he was so good, I found it difficult to watch any other player. Quickly he became one my favorite Angels.

When Ohtani pitches at the Big A, it reminds me of watching Nolan Ryan. When Ryan started, the crowds would grow, and the anticipation of what might be in store was evident. It was electric and unique, and it's the sensation I get when seeing Ohtani perform.

Being an Angels fan means absorbing some heartache, and, yes, I was in the stands for Dave Henderson's two-strike home run in the ninth inning of Game Five of the 1986 American League Championship Series. I actually had a leg over the seating rail near the dugout, ready to storm the field in celebration.

But the Angels fell to the Red Sox, and their first trip to the World Series was delayed until 2002. And, yes, I was in the stands for Scott Spiezio's dramatic home run in Game 6 when the Angels avoided elimination, and I was back the next night when they won their first title.

Those memories are stored with Rod Carew's 3,000th base hit and Ryan setting the single-season strikeout record of 383. As well as recollections of hearing Dick Enberg's smooth voice broadcasting the games and the 1979 season when the Angels won the AL West crown for the first time.

Now in observing Ohtani play with a childlike joy and in a two-way manner every kid does until told otherwise, I think back to those two late Angels who never wore a uniform: Autry and Enberg.

Autry would have cherished Ohtani and likely encouraged his versatility. Remember, Autry was more than just the "Singing Cowboy," as he starred in radio, television, and films and was a successful businessman. One could envision Autry tipping his pristine white cowboy hat in appreciation of Ohtani's varied skills.

And to hear Enberg describing Ohtani's games would have been grand. Enberg was always upbeat and enthusiastic, and he never seemed to be more at home than at the Big A. In some ways, that explains Ohtani, as well. Of course. after one his majestic home runs, Enberg could have delivered an "Oh-tani —Oh My!"

Ohtani's rookie year had plenty of "Oh My" moments. He was electrifying and entertaining, yet humble and gracious. Autry and Enberg would have loved watching him play, and just maybe they did. Not sure if heaven gets cable TV, but if so, Angels games would seem like the appropriate ones to broadcast.

CHAPTER 1

"HI, MY NAME IS SHOHEI OHTANI."

WITH THOSE SIX words, the world's most intriguing baseball player introduced himself to Angels fans on a warm December 9 day in 2017 that will long be remembered in franchise history.

With the Japanese two-way star choosing the Los Angeles Angels over every other major-league club salivating for his services, the Angels had a huge win on a day a baseball wasn't thrown or hit.

Instead, it was the celebration of someone who could do both, and Ohtani handled the initial meet and greet with a mixture of shyness and youthful exuberance.

Ohtani's skill set is unique, although some detractors wonder why he doesn't focus on either hitting or pitching. But what makes him great is that he does both at a high level and has the fortitude to test the status quo that reigns in the majors.

Somewhere along baseball's evolution over the past century, being a specialist became the norm. If you pitched, you didn't hit—or do it very well. If you hit, you didn't pitch—or very seldom.

So Ohtani comes along and carves up that assumption like his inside-out swing when going the opposite way for another base hit.

1

So Ohtani comes along, and he performs—always the biggest factor—at a standard that makes his far-fetched idea resonate.

So what if others told Ohtani he should ditch his challenging endeavor and focus on one or the other?

"It's not like 'I really want to be a pitcher and hit, or that I am a batter who also pitches,'" Ohtani told Kyodo News when preparing for his last season with the Hokkaido Nippon-Ham Fighters. "That's not it. I want to do both.

"Since I began playing ball when I was little, I've wanted to do both. I started playing baseball not thinking, *I really want to be a great player as a pitcher*, or *I want to be a great player as a hitter*.

"I want to bat well. I want to pitch well. That's the desire I've always had."

That drive remains intense despite others throwing shade on his dream of being the first significant two-way player in the majors since Babe Ruth in 1919.

"When it's said, 'If he focused on pitcher, he'd be an even better pitcher so why doesn't he do that?' All I can say is that I really want to be a better hitter," Ohtani said.

Ohtani's greatness isn't restricted to revealing itself when he's wearing a baseball uniform, or dazzling adoring crowds between the lines with a 100-mph fastball or 450-foot home run.

Somewhere in his deepest thoughts, Ohtani decided he was going to be different from others. He had an unrelenting belief in playing baseball his way.

The easier path for him, at some point, would have been to slice his workload in half. Instead, his courage to buck what's considered normal and present a game that few imagined possible was inspiring to others.

Ohtani is popular, to the utmost, for his incredible knack of being able to play the game in a manner not seen in nearly over a century of baseball.

Fans are also drawn to him for what's he's attempting at the major-league level. They applaud him for striving to climb a baseball mountain that maybe only he can see.

What is also appreciated is the way Ohtani pulls all this off.

A father might point out Ohtani's impeccable manners. As is required in the Japanese culture, Ohtani bows when approaching others, and that includes the opposing catcher and umpire when taking his first at-bat in a game.

If Ohtani makes an out, he goes out of his way to retrieve his discarded bat. If he draws a walk, he removes the protective gear from his ankle, elbow, and wrist areas, then he arranges them neatly, waiting for the batboy to arrive.

66

I want to bat well. I want to pitch well. That's the desire I've always had."

—Shohei Ohtani

What baseball player doesn't like sunflower seeds? Not many, and Ohtani lands in the camp that can go through a pack with the best of them.

But don't look for spent seeds under his cleats, and it's not just because he moves around regularly during games.

Instead, it's Ohtani being tidy, not wanting to put an extra burden on a clubhouse attendant to sweep up the mess he left behind. So his discarded seeds go in a cup he keeps nearby.

With Ohtani's path as a two-way player, and the demands and flexibility that are required, some wondered: how he would assimilate in a major-league clubhouse?

Just fine, thank you, and teammate Tyler Skaggs proves it when passing Ohtani's locker and noticing him buried in his iPhone.

Skaggs flicks the back of Ohtani's head in a playful fashion, and the quick smile it brings has them both laughing.

Ohtani has an end locker in the team's west side of the clubhouse and near future Hall of Famer Albert Pujols. There's a concrete partition between the two, but not much else, as it's easy to see Ohtani is among his teammates' favorite targets to joke with.

They rib Ohtani likes one does a little brother, recognizing what he's trying to do and the challenges that come with it. If they can keep him loose, which isn't difficult, his teammates believe they are doing their part, too, in his historic journey.

When Mike Trout, who is across and to the right of Ohtani, starts shooting baskets on the clubhouse's miniature basketball hoop, he baits anyone to compete against him.

That usually gets Ohtani warming up his imaginary jump shot. Although Justin Upton, who's closer to Trout, usually gets the first go at giving Trout the heave-ho in the casual shooting tournament.

It was Trout who was particularly quick to wrap his massive arms around Ohtani. They clicked at spring training camp, as Ohtani would ride shotgun in Trout's golf cart, the one in which he jetted around the Angels' complex.

Both usually sped by with wide grins after their friendship was forged when Trout helped recruit Ohtani with a FaceTime phone call while preparing to get married.

Ohtani was touched, and it was the start of a bond between baseball's best player and its most intriguing one. Instead of being chafed about sharing the spotlight with Ohtani, Trout was cheering for his signing.

Ohtani would later toast Trout—or was that torch? Feeling comfortable with their budding relationship, Ohtani gave Trout the business at his introductory press conference.

When asked why he chose No. 17, Ohtani showed the timing of a stand-up comedian when saying, "I actually wanted No. 27, but someone was wearing that number."

It was among the biggest laugh lines in a city that has produced thousands of smiles. Disneyland is a mile down Katella Street, but on this day, Ohtani made Angel Stadium the happiest place on earth.

Ohtani was set for a season to remember, and he would be living it in an Angels uniform. A franchise that had given its fans the likes of Gene Autry, Bo Belinsky, Dean Chance, Jim Fregosi, Clyde Wright, Alex Johnson, Nolan Ryan, Rod Carew, Reggie Jackson, Vladimir Guerrero, and Trout was adding another impact person to its hallowed alumni.

Those men left their fingerprints on the franchise. As did all the others wearing the Angels uniform with pride, and that goes for late coach Jimmie Reese, a former roommate of Babe Ruth in the 1930s.

Ohtani is trying to duplicate Ruth, and the optimistic and classy Reese, an Angels coach specializing in hitting fungoes until his death at the age of ninety-two, would be the loudest to cheer him on.

But first the roar from the Angels boosters, their offseason suddenly elevated with baseball's biggest signing, had to quiet down at the Ohtani press conference held in front of Angel Stadium. Getting them settled again was a tall task after absorbing the six words the Angels faithful will never forget.

"Hi, my name is Shohei Ohtani."

CHAPTER 2

OHTANI'S YOUTH WAS FILLED WITH BASEBALL

A YOUTHFUL SHOHEI OHTANI'S left-handed swing was far from all wet. Still, the balls that sprung from his bat often splashed down in the river, and that made his coach have a meltdown.

One can imagine a frustrated adult volunteer pleading with the precocious youngster to take the ball the opposite way. The team had a limited supply of baseballs, with many not being dry after the sweet-swinging Ohtani, who started playing baseball in second grade, took batting practice.

Maybe it was around then that the legend and myth, the impossible and the improbable, the unlikely and the unbelievable all started for this Japanese baseball star who has impressed and thrilled fans on both sides of the Pacific Ocean.

Ohtani was born July 5, 1994, in a rural area some 250 miles north of Tokyo. Far from the bright lights of that international city, Ohtani was raised in Oshu, a locale known to be cold in the winter and warm to talking cattle any time of the year.

While the greatness of Ohtani may someday motivate his hometown to create a museum in his honor, please know it will be the second one in town to its original, the Cattle Museum.

Ohtani's parents both participated in sports, supplying their son with some solid athletic genes. His father, Toru, played baseball at the semiprofessional level before a shoulder injury ended his career and he went to work full time at Mitsibushi. Ohtani's mother, Ryuta, was a national badminton team member.

By the time Ohtani enrolled at Hanamaki Higashi High School in the Iwate Prefecture, two things were clear: he had a passion for history and baseball.

Especially baseball.

Ohtani planned to be a star, but first he needed a plan. When a baseball coach suggested to Ohtani and his freshmen teammates to write down their goals, and how to achieve them, they recorded their assumed path to reach their dreams.

Ohtani, who threw right-handed and batted left-handed, had a quest to be selected in the first round and by eight Nippon Professional Baseball teams.

In Japan, multiple organizations can draft a player, then a lottery is held to determine which one would gain his services.

By getting eight teams to show interest, Ohtani would also better flamethrowing southpaw Yusei Kikuchi, who also attended Hanamaki Higashi before going on to play in NPB.

But to cross off that wish, Ohtani had to work diligently with what filled the other 80 boxes on his grid of goals that would lead to his success. Among the traits Ohtani wanted to focus on were mental toughness, physical fitness, nutrition, and building enough strength and accuracy in his right arm to develop a 100-mph fastball.

It was evident Ohtani's talents and determination were a match made in baseball heaven. There was little he couldn't do as he made news while climbing the baseball ladder.

As a sophomore, Ohtani tied future Japanese star and New York Yankees pitcher Masahiro Tanaka's mark by throwing a fastball 150 kph (93.2 mph); and then as a senior, Ohtani did something no other Japanese prep pitcher had accomplished: the radar gun spun to 160 kph (99.4 mph) on one of his offerings.

Ohtani kept checking off items, but it was doubtful he would reach his No. 1 goal of being picked by eight NPB teams.

That was only because the multitalented teenager, who had made the transition from outfielder to pitcher as a freshman, threw NPB a curveball.

Two days before the teams selected their players, Ohtani informed the organizations that he was bypassing NPB and going straight to the major leagues.

❝

It was evident Ohtani's talents and determination were a match made in baseball heaven."

CHAPTER 3

ON SECOND THOUGHT, OHTANI STAYS PUT

SHOHEI OHTANI IS wise beyond his years, both logically and pragmatically. So, when the Ham Fighters presented him a concrete plan of how he could take a shortcut to the majors by playing for them, it piqued his interest.

The Ham Fighters, the only team not scared away by Ohtani's proclamation he was bypassing Nippon Professional Baseball for the majors, drafted him in the first round, and they did their homework.

In painstaking detail, Ham Fighters general manager Masao Yamada showed the dismal success rate of Japanese players going straight to the majors without fine-tuning their skills in NPB.

They convinced an eighteen-year-old Ohtani that if he stayed in his home country, he could hone both his batting and pitching in Japan's top league without being subject to the long bus rides and playing in the less-than-pristine conditions in Major League Baseball's minor leagues.

But the key then, as it would be in 2017 when he picked the Los Angeles Angels when coming to the majors, was Ohtani maintaining his two-way status as a player. Nothing was more important to him as he filled out his 6-foot-4 frame by adding 45 pounds in high school by often devouring 10 bowls of rice a day.

But when Ohtani was selected by the Ham Fighters, he reiterated to the Japanese media that he didn't want to play in NPB.

"I am determined to go to the major leagues," he said. "There isn't any possibility of me accepting the offer."

Ohtani's stance was noteworthy in Japan, according to longtime Kyodo News sportswriter Jim Allen.

"It was big news again when the Fighters drafted him and he wasn't that keen to meet them," Allen said.

But Ohtani relented to break bread with the Ham Fighters' brass, and it was a win for both sides. Once the team's top executives assured Ohtani they were behind his quest to remain a two-way player, there suddenly wasn't only one way to continue his dream of reaching the majors.

Even Ohtani admitted his aspiration of being a two-way player didn't hinge on him, but his bosses.

"I never thought a professional team in Japan would let me do both hitting and pitching before I was drafted, so I can only imagine that it would be a tougher decision for an MLB team to let me do both," Ohtani told Scott Miller of Bleacher Report. "Personally, I would love to do both in the MLB, too, but, ultimately, it is going to be the organization's decision, so I would have to leave that up to them."

But he wasn't leaving anything to chance when deciding to stay in Japan. He needed assurances he could continue to pitch and hit, and when the Ham Fighters agreed to let him do just that, Ohtani put his goal of reaching the majors on hold.

66

I am determined to go to the major leagues."

—Shohei Ohtani

CHAPTER 4

FROM THE PREPS TO THE PROS

THE HAM FIGHTERS got their man in Shohei Ohtani, and he got No. 11 in honor of his pitching idol, Yu Darvish, who had also played for the Ham Fighters and was now with the Texas Rangers.

But exactly what were Ham Fighters getting in Ohtani?

Ohtani, who had played at powerhouse Hanamaki Higashi High School, had wowed the scouts with his velocity in some prestigious prep tournaments in his senior year. But he was far from a finished product as a pitcher, struggling with his control and getting his mechanics right so he could repeat his motion.

"He was just a pitcher who had hit some," said Jim Allen of Kyodo News, who's been writing sabermetric guides about Japanese baseball since 1994 and has covered Ohtani extensively.

When Ohtani arrived in camp, he not only had hitting and pitching on his mind, but he also took grounders at shortstop. He did so with his prized right arm behind his back to protect it from injury.

It was quickly apparent that Ohtani's decision to remain in Japan was the right one. Far from dominating in Nippon Profession Baseball, Ohtani absorbed his lumps and slumps like any other rookie. Still, there were flashes of brilliance that were a clue of what lay ahead for a young man growing into his body and his game.

Ohtani made his professional debut on March 29, 2013; after he struck out in his first at-bat, he collected two hits and had an RBI in the opening-day game against Saitama Seibu Lions ace Takayuki Kishi.

On May 23, Ohtani took the mound for the first time, scattering two runs over five innings when facing the Yakult Swallows. On July 10, he hit his first home run.

Ohtani managed but a .238 batting average with three homers while seeing action in 54 games as an outfielder. But he displayed his gap-to-gap hitting style by notching 15 doubles, only the sixth eighteen-year-old to do so in NPB. His seven assists were the third-best in the Pacific League, with none of the other players reaching that number playing fewer than 101 games.

The pitching side wasn't bad, either. Ohtani won all three of his decisions, with a 4.23 ERA in 13 appearances, which included 11 starts, spread over 61 2/3 innings.

What also drew everyone's attention was his epic batting practice sessions before games. As Ohtani does now, he raised countless eyebrows by producing prodigious home runs while others leaned on the batting cage with amazement.

"He was on the news every night," Allen recalled.

Although it wasn't all positive and despite the naysayers, the Ham Fighters kept their word of helping Ohtani develop both parts of his game.

"There was a lot of criticism of allowing him to hit, since he was a rookie and his .238 batting average was nothing special," Allen said.

He was a gem in the eyes of the fans as they voted him to the Pacific League's All-Star team as a right fielder, despite his missing time with ankle and cheekbone injuries.

But the Ham Fighters knew they had a unique player, and talent, in

Ohtani. Despite a solid but not spectacular debut at the professional level—he was a distant second in the Rookie of the Year balloting to Takahiro Norimoto—Ohtani was confident he was headed in the right direction.

Ohtani found his way to the mound more in his second season, where he went 11–4 in 24 starts. It was clear the consistency of his command was tracking upward. His average of 10.4 strikeouts in nine innings was tops in NPB, and his 179 strikeouts in 155 1/3 innings were the third most in the league.

Batters weren't too thrilled facing Ohtani's fastball, which reached triple digits, and a splitter that mimicked his fastball, only to dive away from the plate at the last moment.

Ohtani the hitter? Yes, he did a bit of that, too. He batted .274 with 10 home runs and 31 RBIs, with an .842 on-base plus slugging percentage.

He also had the flair for the dramatic, which is part of what makes watching Ohtani compelling. In the All-Star Game, he set the NPB record for a Japanese pitcher with an offering clocked at 101 mph. He duplicated the feat in a regular-season game as well, tying Marc Kroon's standard for any pitcher in NPB. During that outing's first inning, eight of Ohtani's 15 pitches were around the century mark.

Ohtani's popularity continued to soar as the nation became transfixed with this player with Hollywood looks and the look of a budding legend. That he was down-to-earth, gracious, and always put his team above his individual feats endeared him to his boosters.

He also displayed skills that weren't common in NPB, which added to his intrigue.

The majority of Japanese pitchers rely on off-speed pitches and deception to be effective.

The 6-foot-4 Ohtani could rear back and be a power pitcher, heaving his offerings at 100 mph.

The majority of Japanese hitters rely on punch singles through the infield or finding a welcoming piece of the field in front of outfielders. Ohtani could do all that, but he also flexed his powerful muscles in blasting tape-measure home runs in the game and batting practice.

When Ohtani smacked his 10th home run on Sept. 7 against the Orix Buffaloes, he was the first Japanese player to reach double figures in wins and home runs, and the first to do it in a top-level league since Babe Ruth in 1918.

Ohtani was selected to Japan's national team, and during a five-game exhibition series against a squad of visiting major-league players, he shined. He had a scoreless inning of work when Japan blanked the MLB players in the first game, and he started Game Five at the Sapporo Dome, which is home to the Ham Fighters. He surrendered one earned run in four innings with seven strikeouts. His fastballs were flirting with the 100s, and the diving characteristics on his splitter were devastating.

The series gave Ohtani positive exposure as he held his own against some of the majors' top players. The secret of Shohei Ohtani, the two-way phenom, was starting to gain international attention.

He also had the flair for the dramatic, which is part of what makes watching Ohtani compelling."

CHAPTER 5

BREAKING OUT ON BOTH SIDES OF HIS GAME

THE INTEREST AROUND Shohei Ohtani was building, and it was easy to see why. He continued his quest to be a two-way player, and he was doing just that with the Ham Fighters.

But in 2015, in his third pro year, it was his growth as a pitcher that was much more significant.

Ohtani was sensational on the mound, as the right-hander went 15–5 with a 2.24 ERA, which led the Pacific League. He had 196 strikeouts in 160 2/3 innings. He set career highs in nearly every individual category with his fastball that hummed by at 100 mph and his secondary pitches that left batters humbled.

"His talents were ridiculous," a National League executive remembered when he scouted Ohtani that season. "With that body, his arm action, and him being an incredible athlete, you knew he was going to keep developing."

Ohtani was selected to the Pacific League's Best Nine squad as a starting pitcher, signifying he was one of the best at that position.

In his other discipline, batting, Ohtani wasn't as proficient. He didn't play as an outfielder, instead getting his hacks as a designated hitter. He managed but a .202 average with five home runs in 109 at-bats.

The following year, it was Ohtani's batting that took center stage. Still, his pitching hardly was shoved aside to the shadows. He starred on the mound, too.

The 2016 campaign was the best of Ohtani's career in Japan, one that he capped by leading the Pacific League's Ham Fighters to their third Japan Series title when they defeated the Hiroshima Toyo Carp in six games, after falling behind 0–2.

His spectacular season not only will be remembered for what he did for the franchise, but it served notice that his quest to play both ways wasn't a ruse.

"

With that body, his arm action, and him being an incredible athlete, you knew he was going to keep developing."
—A National League executive

Ohtani was again a Best Nine selection, this time as both a designated hitter and a pitcher, something that had never been done. In a landslide vote, he was named the Pacific League's MVP.

He batted .322 with 22 home runs and 67 RBIs. As a pitcher, he went 10–4 with 174 strikeouts in 140 innings.

The baseball world was learning the type of amazing player he was. They were discovering Ohtani the person was unique, too.

Despite being one of NPB's biggest stars and more well-known athletes in Japan, Ohtani lived well below the radar. He stayed with the other young Ham Fighters in the team's dormitory. He declined to socialize with his older teammates if drinking alcohol was going be the night's main mission.

Instead of running around town, he often ran back to his room after games and either worked out, played video games, or read books on how he could improve.

"He never went out and lived almost like a monk," said a National League scout. "He didn't care about anything else, it seemed, than getting better at baseball. We heard he lived off a $1,000 allowance every month that his parents gave him. To Shohei, everything revolved around baseball and how to get better at it."

Something that didn't reach 100 percent was Ohtani's ankle. He hurt it when the Ham Fighters beat the Hiroshima Toyo Carp for the Japan Series crown, and it restricted him in 2017 in what would be his final season in Japan. It also prevented him from playing in that year's World Baseball Classic, where Japan, which was one of the event's host countries, finished third behind Puerto Rico and the winner, the United States.

The chatter was already growing that Ohtani would forfeit millions of dollars by not waiting until he was twenty-five years old and head for the majors after the season.

Because Masahiro Tanaka delayed his exit from NPB until he could sign for the most he could gain, the right-hander's deal with the New York Yankees was for seven years and $155 million. That would blow away what Ohtani received, which was a $2.3 million signing bonus and the major-league minimum salary of $545,000.

The big winner, other than the Angels, for securing Ohtani's rights for six seasons was the Ham Fighters. For posting Ohtani's rights and making their star player available, they received $20 million.

Ohtani shrugged about a compromised payday. His goal of being a two-way player in the majors was something that was priceless to him. If Ohtani had to leave some money on the table to reach the majors, that was something for others to worry about.

"That says a lot about him," Angels pitcher Tyler Skaggs told the *New York Times* after he signed with the Angels. "He wants to show us that the money isn't the reason he's here. He just wants to play ball."

CHAPTER 6

AT LONG LAST, "SHO-TIME" WAS HEADING TO THE MAJORS

SHOHEI OHTANI WAS on the market, and his phenomenal two-way game was headed toward the majors.

"I am not a complete player yet, and I want to go to an environment where I can continue to get better," Ohtani said. "I felt the same way when I graduated from high school. And it is my strongest reason for wanting to go now."

And there wasn't a team in the majors that wasn't interested.

Because Ohtani exited Japan before he turned twenty-five, he was restricted by international signing rules on how much money he could accept. So while that was a financial hit to Ohtani, it allowed all 30 teams in the majors to be in the running for his services, as not only big-market teams were suited to facilitate a deal.

How open his prospective employers would be to him continuing his role as a two-way player was questionable. Although there was little doubt that the convoy of executives who had scouted Ohtani in Nippon Professional Baseball and during international tournaments were blown away by his talent.

"It's his combination of skills," a National League general manager said. "He can hit a ball 500 feet, he can throw a ball faster than 100 miles per hour, and he gets down to first base in under four seconds. That's a pretty unique skill set."

But the ever-humble Ohtani wasn't sure if the majors was ready for a pitcher/hitter like him, the first to attempt to do both on a regular basis since Babe Ruth a century ago.

"I don't know if it will be possible, but I want to hear what they say and what kind of situations there might be available," Ohtani told the Associated Press. "Until that process has started, I can't say how it will work out."

Ohtani's five seasons with NPB were a success. After first declining to stay in Japan to play professionally, he signed with the Ham Fighters and directed them to the 2016 Japan Series title.

During his Japanese career, Ohtani went 42–15 with a 2.52 ERA and 624 strikeouts in 543 innings. As a hitter, he slugged 48 homers with 166 RBIs while batting .286.

"Just before I turned professional, I didn't imagine I would be able to do both," Ohtani said. "But since then, the fans have encouraged it, the coaches helped me, and [Ham Fighters] manager [Hideki] Kuriyama made it possible. That has left me with a strong desire to keep doing it, not only for me, but for them."

The ever-humble Ohtani wasn't sure if the majors was ready for a pitcher/hitter like him, the first to attempt to do both on a regular basis since Babe Ruth a century ago."

The Ohtani derby was a full-go, and major-league clubs were pulling out all the stops to get the smooth-swinging, easy-throwing Japanese star to lean in their direction.

The New York Yankees were thought to be a front-runner, as they could play the same card the Ham Fighters did when Ohtani reversed field and decided to stay in Japan after high school instead of going straight to the majors.

With the Ham Fighters, Ohtani was able to follow in the footsteps of his favorite pitcher, Yu Darvish.

If Ohtani went to the Yankees, that was where his hitting idol, Hideki Matsui, was a two-time All-Star and the 2009 World Series MVP.

Matsui, still loyal to the pinstripes, said he was willing to go to bat for the Yankees one more time.

"If he's allowed to come here and the Yankees are interested, then I expect to be involved in that process as maybe trying to convince him or recruit him to the Yankees," Matsui told mlb.com.

Like others close to Japanese baseball, Matsui sees the incredible potential in his budding countryman, especially since he was just twenty-three years old.

"As far as I've seen, [Ohtani's] a good pitcher and he's a good hitter, as well," Matsui said. "He's done well in Japan, so as a baseball fan I'm looking forward to how he's going to do here in the majors and in the US."

Matsui was in Ohtani's corner, but good luck pinning him down on predicting Ohtani's future success as a two-way player. While impressed with what Ohtani had done in Japan, Matsui's 10-year career in the majors gave him pause. After a decade of playing with four different teams, Matsui wasn't certain Ohtani could pull this off.

"As far as I know, I've never really seen a player that performs well as a pitcher and a hitter," Matsui said. "To be honest with you, I really don't know what may come out of it, but I wish him well. If that's something he wants to do and the team wants it, then why not?"

The tug of Ohtani's nostalgia string only went so far. When Ohtani whittled his list to seven teams, the Yankees didn't make the cut.

Instead, the lucky seven consisted of the Los Angeles Dodgers, Los Angeles Angels, Seattle Mariners, Texas Rangers, San Diego Padres, San Francisco Giants, and Chicago Cubs, with Ohtani promising to make a decision quickly.

Those clubs didn't loiter in building their cases on why Ohtani should wear their uniform, with each having a unique angle to entice the world's most compelling player.

Former Japanese star Hideo Nomo threw a no-hitter for the Dodgers. The Angels had the majors' best player in Mike Trout and played in Orange County, where there's a large Asian community. The Mariners count the most famous Japanese player ever, Ichiro Suzuki, among their alumni. The Rangers were the first majors team for Yu Darvish, Ohtani's childhood pitching idol. The Padres, who now employed Nomo, had grown close to Ohtani after the Ham Fighters shared their team's spring training facility in Peoria, Arizona. The Giants also offer a vibrant Asian community spread wide across the Bay Area and the team has something as unique as Ohtani: a Japanese-speaking bench coach and possible manager-in-waiting in Hensley Meulens. Not only could Meulens easily communicate with Ohtani, but Meulens played for three years in NPB and helped lead the Yakult Swallows to the Japan Series title in 1995. The Cubs had a history with Japanese players and would later sign Darvish as a free agent.

Of the finalists, the Rangers ($3.5 million), Mariners ($2.5 million), and Angels ($2.3 million) had the most international pool dollars for Ohtani at their disposal.

Even when considering the $20 million posting fee that went to the Ham Fighters, Ohtani was an incredible bargain. Some speculate a three-time All-Star player coming over from Japan entering his prime years, especially one who both pitched and batted, could fetch a $200 million deal.

The trick, though, was landing Ohtani at any price.

"It was really intense putting together a presentation," said one club official. "We had a plan on how we were going to use him, how we were going to help him improve, what our training schedule was, how we could accommodate his needs—and it all had to be put together really fast."

One of the seven general managers meeting with Ohtani was intrigued by his focus.

"He was very, very serious," he said. "But he was incredibly respectful and had an air of confidence that you respected. You could tell he knows he belongs in the majors and he was wired exactly how you would want someone to be wired at this level. It was clear he wanted to do whatever it took to be best that he could be."

Was the Angels' presentation A-No. 1? Tough to say, and the Angels couldn't care less after Ohtani's representatives gave them the word that their client would be a heaven-sent package for their lineup and rotation.

Otani's agent, Nez Balelo of the Creative Artists Agency, released a statement on December 9 that was met with glee in the Angels offices.

"This morning, after a thorough, detailed process, Shohei Ohtani has decided to sign with the Los Angeles Angels. Shohei is humbled and flattered by all the time and effort that so many teams put into their presentations and sincerely thanks them for their professionalism. In the end, he felt a strong connection with the Angels and believes they can best help him reach his goals in Major League Baseball."

While the Angels celebrated, the teams that finished behind them cursed their fate.

"We're disappointed we weren't Shohei Ohtani's choice but wish him the best in Anaheim," Rangers general manager Jon Daniels told mlb.com. "He impressed us on and off the field at every turn. However, had he asked our opinion, we would have suggested the National League."

At least Daniels maintained his sense of humor. More than eight months after Ohtani's decision to take his talents to the Angels, one general manager of a West Coast club remains crestfallen.

"He would have been a perfect fit for our team, and we did everything we thought possible to make it happen," he said, electing to remain unnamed. "It's still kind of hard to talk about because of his unique skills and his incredible mental component to be the best.

"I guess ultimately we will never know why he made his decision, but it remains a sensitive subject to us."

That he was heading to the Angels for the next six seasons was a godsend to their franchise and fans.

"I think he felt that there was a family-like atmosphere [with the Angels] and something that he was wanting to and willing to be a part of for a lot of years to come," Angels general manager Billy Eppler told the team's flagship radio station, AM 830 KLAA. "I think it was his comfort level with us and not only just the plan that we put together for him, but just the overall vibe of the organization."

But Eppler kept his winning template close to his vest. What he did reveal was that Ohtani would have a big say in how he could maximize his production and participation.

"I'm not going to dive into specifics on the plan, only because the plan that we put forth for him was derived off his historical workloads in [Nippon Professional Baseball]," Eppler said. "The most important participant in the plan, it's going to be Shohei. It's going to be how he is accustomed to developing and how he is accustomed to his own workload management. He's going to really be an active participant in this plan."

The blueprint for Ohtani would be constructed and executed. But first came a press conference the following day under the massive Angels hats in front of Angel Stadium, where Ohtani's newest boosters would see him in the flesh for the first time.

All were invited to the surreal press conference, including who many considered to be the most intriguing baseball player in the world.

CHAPTER 7

TIME FOR LA TO INTRODUCE ITS HEAVEN-SENT ANGEL

SHOHEI OHTANI HIT a home run in his introductory press conference.

Or did he toss a no-hitter?

Either way, or both ways, the two-way star from Japan was pitch-perfect while being front-and-center as the Angels greeted him with a rousing welcome in front of Angel Stadium.

It had been a whirlwind week for the Angels as they crossed their fingers and dotted every '*i*' in their presentation to Ohtani on Monday, December 4, in hopes of convincing the Japanese Babe Ruth to select their team over six others.

On Friday morning, they received word from Ohtani's representative, Nez Balelo of Creative Artists Agency, that his client, who later said he felt "a connection with the Angels," was looking forward to becoming one.

Then Saturday arrived, and a joyous press conference at Angel Stadium few ever envisioned played out just east of the Big A and in the shadow of the bright red Angels hats.

When Ohtani spoke, he was red, too, being a tad embarrassed.

"This is the first time I've been talking in front of such a big crowd that I actually forgot what I was going to say," Ohtani said. "You guys are making me all nervous."

Ohtani's remark was met with laughs as he poked fun of himself while trying to deflect some of the relentless praise he was being showered with.

Although when Victor Rojas, the team's radio voice and the event's master of ceremonies, rattled off Ohtani's accomplishments in Japan, many were hearing them for the first time.

Angels fans were ecstatic about getting Ohtani, but some of them weren't familiar with his game or just how ultratalented the lanky 6-foot-4 man with a shy smile and wispy black hair really was.

They quickly learned that Ohtani was humble and had good manners, too.

He thanked the Angels front office and its high-level executives. When it came time to salute the manager, he was referred to as "Mr. Mike Scioscia."

"I also would like to thank my parents, my family, my teammates that I played with in Japan, the coaching staffs, and all the Japanese fans," he said.

Some praise should probably head Mike Trout's way. The Angels' two-time American League MVP took time from his wedding week to lob Ohtani a recruitment FaceTime call during their meeting with Ohtani.

"He mentioned that he was preparing for his wedding, so he couldn't come out to the presentation, which I totally understand," said Ohtani, whose bachelor status isn't lost on his legions of female fans. "I want him to have a happy life with his wife, and I look forward to seeing him soon.

"He basically explained to me how great the Angels were, how they have a great clubhouse, and how he would enjoy having me here. And I just took those words to heart and I'm here."

The thought of that already had Scioscia considering how Ohtani will be used.

"We definitely plan on him being a two-way player," he said. "There is no doubt about that.

"With Shohei obviously there is a lot on his plate, a lot on our plate and we will work through it one step at a time and make sure this guy is as good a pitcher as he can be and as good a hitter as he can be."

For the newest Angel with the baby face, that sounds a lot like doing things like Babe Ruth did nearly a century ago.

No one has done them since until Ohtani threw a fastball past conventional baseball wisdom and knocked status quo out of the park while playing for the Ham Fighters in Japan.

"I'm honored to be compared to Babe Ruth, but in no way do I think I am at his level," Ohtani said. "Today I think is the real starting point for me, and I just hope to get as close to him as possible."

Added Scioscia: "I don't think we've seen a pitcher of his caliber in our organization for a long time, and that will support whatever he can do in the batter's box."

66

We definitely plan on him being a two-way player. There is no doubt about that."

—Mike Scioscia

Ohtani's game requires an out-of-the-box philosophy, and he felt the Angels would support him best as he shakes up the grand old game.

"I entered this process with a very open mind," Ohtani said. "I wanted to hear what every team had to offer and give everyone a chance and at the end of the day I decided to pick the Angels."

That tickles the Angels as they secure a player oozing with talent for six seasons and he's just twenty-three years old.

"First of all, in no way do I think I am a complete player," Ohtani said. "We win championships not with one player but with a team and teammates. I think the fans are the ones that are going to help me become a better player."

That brought another cheer, and it felt like Christmas had come early to those wearing Los Angeles Angels gear. The more Ohtani talked, the more those in attendance embraced this multiskilled player with a gracious personality, the likes of which they had never seen before.

Ohtani felt out of place, too.

"I am used to standing in front of big crowds, I'm just not used to talking in front of big crowds," Ohtani said. "Obviously I'm very nervous, I am just more worried that everyone understands what I'm saying."

His message was coming through cleanly. Ohtani was as happy to pin his hopes of being a two-way star in the majors with the Angels as the Angels were pleased to pin their wings on him.

CHAPTER 8

SPRING TRAINING DELIVERS MORE QUESTIONS THAN ANSWERS

THE TWO ANGELS boosters were standing in the concourse behind the plate at Tempe Diablo Stadium as their favorite team played an exhibition game on a delightful March day in the Valley of the Sun.

One fan wore a worn T-shirt highlighting the Angels' 2002 World Series title.

His buddy was sporting a sparkling new T-shirt with "Ohtani" blazoned on the back of it, just above the Japanese star's No. 17. He forgot to remove the price tag of his recent purchase, and during the course of their conversation, both of them were getting their two cents in.

"I'm not so sure about this Shohei Ohtani guy," the one in the fall classic shirt said.

"Be patient," his colleague quickly added, as he buried his souvenir's receipt in his pocket. "It's still spring training."

Or was it a spring that was trying the Angels' patience with their two-way star, as his play was nearly a one-way street filled with potholes and obstacles?

31

Ohtani was the talk of the spring in Arizona, but his game wasn't rising. After five years of being a standout in Nippon Professional Baseball, where he was an All-Star in three of his seasons, he was getting pushed around at the plate and pummeled on the mound during the Cactus League.

The Japanese version of Babe Ruth left many Angels fans curious about what this Ohtani hysteria was all about.

It was his debut outing on February 24 in which it became clear Ohtani, like every other rookie, would have an adjustment period.

The Angels pitcher with a worldwide appeal and throngs of international media tracking his every step looked pretty average. Against the Milwaukee Brewers, he allowed two runs (one earned) and two hits, which included a home run by Keon Broxton, while recording four outs over 31 offerings.

Then in his second start in Arizona, Ohtani was scorched for seven runs by the Colorado Rockies, surrendering two tape-measure home runs to Ian Desmond and Nolan Arenado on March 16.

In two brief appearances in which he got a combined eight outs, it was clear Ohtani was out of sorts. Or was he just playing coy?

Reporters covering the Angels were straightforward with a question that seemed out of the question just over three months ago when Los Angeles introduced Ohtani at a press conference, hinting that he was about to revolutionize the major leagues.

They poked at manager Mike Scioscia, asking if Ohtani would even break camp with the big club.

"I'm not going to get into roster decisions," Scioscia told *USA Today*. "I can only say that Shohei's talent is real. Obviously, we believe in it. We anticipate him being ready to both pitch and hit when the season starts, and we're going to work hard to reach that goal from now until we start the season."

It was clear Ohtani's indoctrination to the majors wasn't going well. But all was swell in Scioscia's eyes, and he's the one that counts. The veteran skipper attributed Ohtani's struggles to mechanical errors that had his delivery off-kilter.

"We're not measuring him on ERA," Scioscia said. "We're not measuring him on how many guys he strikes out. There's different components of the lens we're looking at, and it's all about that process."

Before facing the Rockies, Ohtani had tuned up against the Tijuana Toros of the Mexican League and given up six runs and five hits in three innings.

On March 2, when competing against the Brewers' "B" team, Ohtani showed his stuff in spurts, charged with two runs in 2 2/3 innings.

Ohtani also wasn't putting much of a jolt into baseballs as a hitter. In his first 11 plate appearances, Ohtani's long, lengthy swing produced one hit.

Ohtani's ho-hum start in his quest to mimic Babe Ruth as a two-way player was like feeding candy bars to Ohtani's detractors. They pointed to his sweeping cut, diminished velocity—after throwing 102 mph in Japan, he sat in the high-90s—and the elevated level of competition for the reasons why Ohtani was out of his league.

But Mark Gubicza, a former major-league pitcher covering the Angels for Fox Sports West TV, wasn't covering his eyes in disgust. In fact, he saw what the casual fan possibly missed.

"I heard and read all the negative vibes and reviews about him in spring training, but I wasn't buying them," he said. "I saw pretty much every one of his games, and I remember one inning he threw the ball like 97, 98 and he was just starting out the game and it's hard to get that type of velocity.

"Then he threw a couple wicked sliders and then a couple of good sliders and I said, 'Wow, this guy is legit.'

"Obviously he had some tough innings down there, but I saw enough swings and misses that I thought he would be special."

But the spring represented a slow start, although the Angels and

Ohtani didn't remove their facade that everything would work itself out in due time.

The clock was ticking fast toward opening day, and Ohtani was still searching for answers at the plate and on the mound. He would get one more start before the Angels' spring fling in Arizona was over, with Ohtani going against minor-league hitters. It was another appearance against younger players, the ones Ohtani, if he's what was advertised, should dominate.

But in an 85-pitch performance, his fastball was erratic, and that led to five walks, a hit batter, and two offerings that found the back-stop for wild pitches.

Spring was over, and Ohtani looked like he needed a break, not an invitation to join a major-league team embarking on a 162-game season. He finished with a 27.00 ERA in his two starts against major-league teams, with a .125 batting average.

"He's working on some things, he'll be fine," Scioscia said calmly.

Ohtani, as well, wasn't rattled when reviewing his spring results.

"I feel like I've done everything I can to get ready for opening day, and I felt like I've done everything 100 percent," Ohtani told report-ers. "But it's hard.

"Every other year, even in Japan, I was never 100 percent [ready] on opening day, so it's going to go gradually into the season. I think it's going to be the same this year."

Once the regular-season games were on tap, Ohtani wouldn't have the luxury of trying to retire players minus major-league service time. Some wondered if Ohtani should have tested his wares against sea-soned opponents.

"Of course, in a perfect world, I would have liked to face more major-league hitters, but it's more than that," he said. "It's also about me making adjustments with the mound and the ball and all that. It didn't really matter who I faced. I just had to check with my own stuff, mechanics, [and] timing."

A National League scout had his own checks-and-balances system, and all indications to him were that Ohtani's performances weren't cause to punch the panic button.

"He's got No. 1 starter stuff and a middle-of-the-lineup bat," he said.

Still, the baseball purists pointed to Ohtani's numbers and chuckled loudly, hoping someone would inquire what the cackling was about and they could say, "I told you so about Ohtani!"

Meanwhile, Ohtani and Scioscia didn't bend in their belief that the Japanese star's spring training was much ado about nothing.

"Of course I still believe I'm going to have good results," Ohtani told mlb.com. "I believe in myself and I'll keep working hard every day and the results will follow."

Scioscia nodded in agreement, and despite Ohtani's underwhelming numbers—he also had zero extra-base hits in 32 at-bats—everything was groovy in the Angels orbit.

"He's confident he is going to find it," Scioscia said. "Just as we're confident he's going to find it."

Those two Angels fans who started the chapter arguing about Ohtani? They agreed to disagree, by playing it smart and letting the regular-season results sway their arguments.

CHAPTER 9

MARCHING IN WITH A ROAR

March 29

Shohei Ohtani was a major leaguer, with the Angels giving him the news he had made the roster two days earlier. Ohtani had struggled in spring training, and his addition to the 40-man roster wasn't a slam dunk.

Nonetheless, it took Ohtani about 24 seconds to get his first knock. Serving as the Angels' designated hitter, he stroked the initial pitch he saw from righty Kendall Graveman for a single in a 6–5 loss in 11 innings.

"That's probably an at-bat I'm not going to forget for the rest of my life," Ohtani told the *Orange County Register*.

It was a day Ohtani's teammate, Mike Trout, would just as soon throw back, as he went hitless in six at-bats for the first time in a game.

But Ohtani's debut eclipsed Trout's abnormality as the two-way player's career in the majors had finally pushed off from the dock. And he did it with a nod to his Japanese heritage as he joined countrymen Hideki Matsui, Kazuo Matsui, Tsuyoshi Shinjo, and Kosuke Fukudome in getting a hit in their first MLB at-bats. Hideki Matsui was Ohtani's hitting idol during his youth.

But manager Mike Scioscia wasn't concerned about those former Japanese standout players. Instead, he was standing on the top step of the Angels dugout, enjoying "Sho-Time."

"I thought Shohei was fine," Scioscia told mlb.com. "Getting in the batter's box, I thought he had some good swings. Got the base hit, hit a couple balls hard to second, so just out of the chute, it's good for him to get out there. I know he'll continue to improve."

As he continues a path that hasn't been taken on a consistent basis in nearly a century. For Ohtani's talents to be best utilized, he won't hit in games in which he pitches (which prevents him from starting at National League stadiums) and in the days preceding and following his outings.

April 1

No kidding, the Angels' designated hitter three days ago left his bat in the rack. Instead, he grabbed his glove and headed to the bump in the middle of the diamond at Oakland-Alameda County Coliseum.

Shohei Ohtani was there, on the mound as a pitcher, and perhaps, a la Gertrude Stein, it was appropriate that Oakland was the venue. The historic journey that Ohtani had embarked on was getting ready to reveal the pitching side of No. 17 against the Athletics.

After a rocky spring training when he had trouble getting minor leaguers out, Ohtani's debut as a starter was a steady patch of smooth road for most of his outing. Ohtani allowed three runs, but on only three hits over six innings—one was Matt Chapman's three-run homer—in pacing the Angels to a 7–4 victory.

He struck out six and gathered steam as the game progressed, retiring 14 of the final 15 batters he faced.

"Personally, I feel like I got off to a good start, and obviously the team went 3–1 on the first road trip, so I'm very happy with the results," Ohtani told the Associated Press.

Ohtani, who walked one, made but one glaring mistake against the A's. That's when Chapman pounded his blast in the second, which was the lone Oakland offensive highlight against the right-hander with the explosive fastball and darting splitter.

"He used everything," manager Mike Scioscia said. "Outside of maybe one stretch of three hitters in the second inning, that's about as well as you could pitch."

The game never seemed too big for Ohtani, who was calm throughout his outing. Of course, with the way he was pitching, there was little to fret about.

"Shohei has shown great poise in everything he's done—the way he's practiced, the adjustments he's made at the plate when he's swinging the bat," Scioscia added. "I think that's going to be one of his strengths moving on."

In the present, it was quite an event. With shouts of "Oh-tan-i!" going up at a road game when he took the mound, it was "Sho-Time" indeed. Ohtani's deliveries reached 100 mph in the first inning, and he kept Oakland at bay for most of his 92-pitch effort.

Not since Babe Ruth pulled it off in 1919 had a player started on opening day in a nonpitching role, then started on the mound in the first 10 games.

April 3

Shohei Ohtani had one shot at his first impression with Angels fans, and he supplied one to highlight his debut at Angel Stadium, his home for the next six years.

The Angels hit nearly one homer for every season the team had secured Ohtani's rights. Instead, they fell one short with five, but with one of them courtesy of Ohtani, it made this game special.

In his first at-bat, he went yard with a three-run homer off Josh Tomlin. That put the bow on a six-run first inning, with the Angels crowd of 35,007 in full throat and soaking in just what might be possible with Ohtani on the team.

That wasn't Ohtani's only contribution in the 13–2 win over the

Cleveland Indians. He added two singles to his day when the baseball world again did a double take when watching the Angels highlights.

Ohtani had to look twice, too, when his first-inning long fly left his bat at 104.5 mph.

"When I hit it, I thought it was going to be off the wall, so I was running hard," he told mlb.com. "But I'm glad it cleared the fence."

When he got back to the dugout, his teammates cleared a wide path. Instead of greeting Ohtani with joy, they gave him the traditional silent treatment befitting a rookie who hit his first home run.

Ohtani got handshakes from René Rivera, who was up next, then Zack Cozart, who was on deck. Otherwise, the Angels were suddenly as quiet as those who had stated in spring training that Ohtani was all hype with little hope of succeeding in the majors.

With no one extending congratulations, Ohtani walked eight steps down the dugout giving up imaginary high fives. Then all at once, the dugout exploded with enthusiasm as players and coaches saluted their skilled rookie.

At Mike Trout's bequest, Ohtani climbed back out of the dugout and doffed his hat to those in attendance, in what was likely the first of many Ohtani curtain calls.

The Angels are ecstatic they didn't listen to the doubters after Ohtani's scratchy spring training. Ohtani has shown in a very small sample size that he's got a big-time skills.

"You didn't have any naysayers wearing an Angels uniform," Scioscia stressed. "I'll let the other people speak for whatever they think."

Ohtani is the first player to notch a win in one game, then homer while not a pitching in his next game, since Babe Ruth in 1921.

April 4

The calendar didn't read "Groundhog Day," but one can't fault Angels fans for relishing Shohei Ohtani's repeat performance.

Ohtani hit his second home run in as many games as the Angels got past the Cleveland Indians, 3–2, in 13 innings to secure its first home series of the season.

That this one came against Corey Kluber, a two-time Cy Young Award winner, added another chapter to Ohtani's amazing start.

"That ball is out of here," screamed Terry Smith, the Angels' radio broadcaster in describing the game-tying, 400-foot blast to center field. "Holy Mackerel!"

Holy Ohtani took Kluber's pitch on the outer half of the plate and flicked his powerful wrists in sending it over the fence in the opposite direction.

"Corey Kluber is not a guy that gives up a lot of home runs, and he got a ball out over the plate and Shohei got a hold of it," Scioscia told mlb.com.

With the crowd going berserk, Ohtani's teammates played it straight. Mike Trout removed Ohtani's helmet when he returned from his tour of the bases, and unlike the silent treatment he got with his first home run, Ohtani was engulfed in backslaps, high-fives, and hugs.

"Offense is really almost constant failure because hitting a baseball is one of the hardest things to do in sports," second baseman Ian Kinsler said. "Then to square up against a Cy Young Award winner that early in his career, and to never have seen the guy before? It was a great at-bat."

But Ohtani told the Associated Press that he was just looking for a knock that would slice the Angels' deficit in half. Instead, his swing knotted the score at 2–2.

"There was a runner on second base, so I was just trying to get a base hit and keep my swing compact, and it ended up clearing the fence," he said. "I think everything is going really well right now. I'm off to a good start."

Ohtani will let others ease into the season as he continues to contribute in nearly every way imaginable. The rookie has either got a hit or collected a pitching victory in each game he's played in the majors.

April 6

Shohei Ohtani, still hitting from the No. 8 hole, went 1-for-4 against the Athletics. But on closer inspection, he was actually 3-for-3: he swatted a home run in his third straight game.

This time, Ohtani helped fuel an Angels comeback win as they rallied from being down six runs to beat Oakland, 13–9. His third homer on the season landed in the water filling the faux rock foundation in center field as the spectators erupted in joy.

That was nothing fake about Ohtani's blast. It rocketed off his bat at 112.4 mph and went an estimated 449 feet. It was the hardest and longest fly ball struck by an Angel this season. He became the first Angels rookie to homer in his first three home games.

"It's getting old," joked shortstop Andrelton Simmons to mlb.com. "No, but it's really cool to see him swing the bat that well. I'm happy for him. I think we all are. He has big power, and he's showing it."

Shohei showing off? Maybe, and the Angels couldn't be happier.

Their emerging star is the first American League player to homer in three straight games in the same season that he started a game as a pitcher since Babe Ruth in 1930. With three homers, Ohtani had more than three teams—the Detroit Tigers, Kansas City Royals, and Miami Marlins.

"Oh-tan-i! Oh-tan-i!" is becoming the go-to chant for Angels backers, as each of his at-bats transfixes everyone in the stadium and both dugouts.

While his quest to become a two-way player in the majors makes him captivating to watch, his production solidifies how special he could be.

He's now 7-for-18 (.389) with three homers and seven RBIs in his four starts as designated hitter. Ohtani is the first American League player to collect a home run and at least two RBIs in each of his first three home games since RBIs became an official statistic in 1920.

April 8

Heaven is supposed to be perfect, and for six innings the newest Angel was just that.

Shohei Ohtani, again showing his flair for the dramatic, took a perfect game into the seventh inning of his third start in the majors. With a rowdy gathering of 44,742—more than attended on opening day—cheering his every pitch, Ohtani flirted with baseball immortality as he stymied the Oakland Athletics for the second time in a week.

"That's as good a game as you're ever going to see pitched," manager Mike Scioscia said in his postgame briefing with reporters. "To pitch as well as he did through seven innings is not easy. He's got great stuff and made some terrific pitches."

Ohtani didn't allowed a baserunner for 6 1/3 innings until Marcus Semien singled, and he collected 12 strikeouts.

That pushed his strike out total to 18 in his two starts, and to illustrate the dominating fashion of his two-strike pitches, all 18 of the strikeouts came on swings-and-misses. His lively fastball and elusive splitter were nearly unhittable.

"His splitter just kind of drops off the table," Angels infielder Zack Cozart told mlb.com· "[It] looks like a strike I feel like almost every time, but it never is. It just drops below the zone. That's how it comes out, the same as his fastball. It makes it tough as a hitter."

But what makes that pitch so bewildering is that Ohtani can pinpoint his fastball as if he were throwing darts.

"Without fastball command, people wouldn't have been swinging at his splitter," catcher Martin Maldonado said. "I think the ability to throw the fastball wherever he wanted made the hitter feel pressure to swing at his splitter."

Ohtani was tested in the seventh after a single and a walk, which prompted pitching coach Charles Nagy to stroll to the mound. Their brief conversation resulted in Ohtani getting slugger Khris Davis on a fielder's choice, then an animated Ohtani struck out Matt Olson on a full-count splitter, his 91st and final offering of the afternoon.

"I wanted to keep a clean zero on the board," Ohtani said. "One hit would have been two runs—that's a huge difference, I wanted that strikeout and I got it."

In running his record to 2–0, Ohtani became the first player in the majors with two wins and three home runs in his team's first 10 games since Jim Shaw did it for the Washington Senators in 1919.

Ohtani was the third player to homer in three consecutive games and record a double-digit strikeout performance in the same season. Babe Ruth was the first player to do it in 1916.

April 17

There was a buzz at Angel Stadium, never mind that it was a school night and the balmy summer evenings had yet to envelop the team's baseball digs in Orange County.

The Angels had just completed a 6–0 road trip by winning their seventh straight game, raising their record to 13–3. That's the best start in team history, and when combined with Ohtani's third start and the dreaded Boston Red Sox in town, it's easy to see what all the commotion was about.

When the turnstiles quit humming, 44,882 tickets were collected for the Angels' second-biggest crowd since the venue was refigured in 1998. It was the team's first Tuesday night sellout in four years, in a game that again drew more spectators than opening day.

Ohtani was eager to start at home after he was scratched when the Angels and Royals were rained out three days earlier.

"The fans, their cheers, and their support is going to help me pitch," he told the *Los Angeles Times*. "I'm going to try and use the momentum once again."

But then the pregame hype subsided, and the Red Sox bats started to highjack Ohtani's pitches. Leadoff batter Mookie Betts collected the first of his three home runs when crushing Ohtani's 97 mph fastball, and the Angels weren't worth a hill of beans in a 10–1 laugher.

There were few smiles from Ohtani, either.

After turning the baseball world on its ear in the opening three weeks, Ohtani returned to earth. He didn't make it to the third inning, forced to the showers by a blister on the middle finger of his throwing hand.

The Ohtani story had flipped as he surrendered three runs on four hits in recording six outs.

"It definitely had an effect on his command, especially his off-speed pitches," manager Mike Scioscia said afterward in a crowded media session. "He got through two innings, but we don't want it to get any worse."

Beaten up by a rough outing, Ohtani said that the blister first appeared in his previous start and became aggravated against the Red Sox, the only team with a better record than the Angels.

"They took a look at it and felt it would be fine for today," Ohtani said. "But under the high intensity of the game, it didn't hold up too well."

It wasn't a new ailment for Ohtani, as he had battled skin irritations throughout his Japanese career. And while he was confident it wouldn't be a long-term injury, he was also cognizant of the baseball calendar.

"It's a long season and it's early in the season, so I'm being really cautious with it," Ohtani said.

But he was not overly concerned.

"I have a decent idea how long it will take to recover and heal," he said. "Usually in Japan I would pitch without it fully healing. I think it will be something like that this time around."

He didn't make it around the Red Sox order more than once before being relieved. Ohtani lasted but 12 batters, as baseball proved once again there are two types of players: a humble one or one about to be humbled.

"Obviously I'm not going to be at the top of my game for every start," Ohtani said. "For half of my starts I won't be at the top of my game. I need to learn more and get better."

The Red Sox discovered quickly they could ignore Ohani's wipeout splitter, as it didn't have the bite, depth, and location as in his previous two starts. In those outings, Ohtani recorded 18 strikeouts, and all came on swings-and-misses.

On his 66 offerings to Boston hitters, they swung-and-missed on only three pitches. Ohtani had but one strikeout on a checked swing by J. D. Martinez.

"My splitter, I didn't have good command of that," Ohtani said. "My fastball, I couldn't feel it off my fingertips. My slider, I couldn't feel it."

April 24

Houston had a problem, and it was because of Shohei Ohtani.

Ohtani flicked away concerns about the blister that chased him from his previous start as he helped beat the Astros, 8–7. He wasn't around for a decision after the Angels rallied, but his verdict was nonetheless a winning one.

"I felt a lot better than the last outing," he said. "It pretty much had no bad effects on me tonight."

That was good news to the Angels as they exhaled a tad. Often blisters can be troublesome, but not if the skin rejuvenates quickly.

Ohtani rebounded from his shellacking by the Red Sox with 5 1/3 innings over which he allowed four runs, striking out five and walking four.

After getting 86'd by the powerful Red Sox, Ohtani threw 98 pitches to the Astros, with six offerings speeding past the 100-mph mark. Ohtani was throwing harder than in previous outings, and that didn't go unnoticed.

Neither did home plate umpire Eric Cooper's unforgiving strike zone. Some opined that his reluctance to raise his right arm on a handful of Ohtani pitches led to the five walks and a pitch count that had manager Mike Scioscia reluctantly reaching for the bullpen phone.

"Good eye today," he said of Houston's hitters, his tongue in cheek.

Ohtani pointed to his right arm, instead.

"I couldn't develop the kind of rhythm I wanted," he said. "It's really a great lineup."

Ohtani showed flashes of greatness, but it was an up-and-down start, his fourth in the majors. But unlike the others, it came with relief, as the Angels' emerging star KO'd his blisters, if not the defending world champions.

April 27

If Shohci Ohtani could make it in New York, he could make it anywhere. But when he declined the Yankees' offseason overtures to slap on the pinstripes, Ohtani showed them what they were missing in their first meeting.

Ohtani stroked his fourth home run, this one coming off righty Luis Severino, one of the American League's top pitchers, in the Yankees' 4–3 triumph in 10 innings. He turned on a thigh-high 97-mph fastball and deposited it deep into the right-field seats.

But Ohtani would have just one more at-bat in the series opener. He sprained his left ankle sprinting down the line when trying to beat out a grounder in the fifth inning.

The mild tweak of Ohtani's ankle, which helped keep him out of the lineup the next two games, did nothing to knock Scioscia from his core belief: Ohtani's stellar first month in the majors was no fluke.

"One thing just in watching Shohei is you see that his talent is real," Scioscia said. "There is no questioning his ability, I don't think there is any questioning the impact on our club, and we are excited to have him."

NAGY JUGGLES ASSIGNMENTS TO ACCOMMODATE OHTANI

Charles Nagy settles in behind the wheel for his 120-mile round-trip drive to Anaheim, where baseball's most intriguing pitcher is reporting to work.

Nagy, the Angels pitching coach who resides south in North San Diego County, doesn't mind his trek to Orange County.

"It's not that far," he said.

But this year is different with the Angels' rookie pitcher from the Far East: Shohei Ohtani.

Ohtani, in his first season after starring in Japan, is not only under Nagy's tutelage as a pitcher. The right-handed hurler is also a left-handed hitter, and yeah, he does both equally well.

"He's been great," said Nagy, who won 129 games in the majors. "He's a happy kid, easygoing. He loves baseball, you can tell."

And baseball is loving him right back, embracing the nuances of the sport's first two-way player since Babe Ruth pulled it off nearly a century ago.

But when Ruth was pitching and hitting, the Yankees didn't have a pitching coach. Mike Scioscia, the Angels manager, has the luxury of leaning on Nagy.

With Ohtani, Nagy has had to tinker with a six-man rotation that features one more starter than other teams. Nagy also has to balance when Ohtani is practicing hitting with his drills to hone his pitching.

Ohtani doesn't bat in games he pitches, or the day before or after his outing. He doesn't pitch in the games in which he hits.

Nagy is responsible for Ohtani making sure he gets his work in between starts, while also juggling a rotation that was derailed by injuries.

"The life of a major-league pitching coach encompasses a lot of stuff," Scioscia said. "Luckily, Charles is good at it.

"Shohei's history says he has pitched sometimes on five, six days rest, sometime longer, in Japan. We hope that we come to a point this season that if we have a six-man rotation, he will be able to pitch on the sixth day instead of the seventh day. But we'll see as we approach that."

Nagy was better than good through his 14 years in the majors, his last one being with the San Diego Padres in 2003. He was a three-time All-Star, and he pitched in two World Series with the Cleveland Indians.

Ohtani had kind words for Nagy.

"He has really good eyes, and he has been watching me," Ohtani said. "He has been giving me advice and has been a huge help to me."

Nagy connects with his pitchers because he's walked in their cleats.

"He always brings a positive mind-set," said Angels starter Nick Tropeano. "There are always going to be those rough outings that you have, but he will be there with that smile and that learn-and-forget mentality and that's what you need."

What the Angels have required from their staff is flexibility because of the uniqueness of Ohtani. And much of the responsibility of making sure it goes smoothly lies with Nagy.

"With Ohtani, he is a different type of player," Tropeano said. "We don't really know how to work a two-way guy like that. I think the whole coaching staff, but Nagy especially, has been doing well with it.

"We're going with a six-man rotation, and that is pretty uncharted water there. But when you have a talent like Ohtani, you aren't going to pass that up. You'll make the adjustment."

Ohtani has had his share of the unknown, which isn't lost on Nagy.

"It's a different challenge with him," Nagy said. "But he has his challenges. It's a new league, it's a new everything for him.

"So we just kind of help him out a bit and pretty much let him adapt as much as possible by just trying to talk to him and work around his schedule.

"He comes out when his time permits, and we make sure we are available, that we are here. It's not crazy times or anything like that. He's pitching once a week now, and he throws a little on the side twice a week."

Nagy slides his car seat back after the game and heads home to complete the second half of his two-way trip to the Big A. The game's only two-way player, Ohtani, will be waiting tomorrow for his return.

"You would have thought it would have happened sooner," Nagy said. "But he came over highly touted in both regards. And just as a fan of the game, I'm just watching and hoping he succeeds, like everybody else."

If so, it will be a team effort for Ohtani and others.

Nagy is the man tweaking schedules and starters. When Ohtani had to skip a start against the Baltimore Orioles because of a sore ankle, the rotation was altered again.

"It's just about keeping the guys informed," Nagy said. "The other four or five guys we have in the rotation we have to make sure they are on schedule and they know when they are pitching and what they need to do to get ready for those starts."

Being at the start of something as special as Ohtani's first season in the majors is worth it.

"Going into it we talked to [the starters] before the season and spring training," Nagy said. "Flexibility was the main word that was thrown around, and these guys all bought into it out of the gate.

"They want to win and they want us to succeed as a team. They know having Ohtani is going to help us do that, so they are going to be flexible."

Nagy is a good listener, but his main job is putting his trained eye on hurlers. What's he seen from Ohtani?

"His mechanics are pretty flawless, they are great," he said. "Then he's in the upper 90s with the fastball and he has a good curve and a good slider. And him having his phenomenal splitter doesn't hurt."

The question remains whether Ohtani can split time between standing at the plate and aiming for it. Nagy has been around enough to know nothing is guaranteed.

"I don't see why he can't do it and hopefully he can," Nagy said. "But it's a long season so we'll see what toll it takes on him, and as time goes on, we will see how he fares."

The Angels will see how hitters will compensate when batting against Ohtani. They will cheat on some pitches, guess on others, and study Ohtani to find any flaw not yet deciphered.

"He's going to have to make adjustments, but he is a student of the game," Nagy said. "He knows what he can and can't do and what he needs to do. And as we go down the road and he has to make some adjustments, he will."

Life in America is different for Ohtani, but he's trying to fit in. He hangs with the pitchers, because some of the time, he's just like them.

"They all sit together during the games in the dugout, but obviously he is a little bit different because he may be hitting that day or doing something else," Nagy said. "If he has questions, he knows where to go to."

Surprisingly, he grasps the language enough to get a reply.

"We have a translator, but he knows a little more English and it's been OK so far," Nagy said of the communication gap. "[Ohtani] also understands a little bit more English than I understand Japanese. He understands what we are doing when we talk about things."

Ohtani was the focal point of the baseball universe in the season's first month. Against the A's, he took a no-hitter into the seventh inning, so is this the same guy who scuffled in spring training?

Yep, the same humble, happy-go-lucky rookie with a steady smile and a steely resolve to improve in both areas of his game.

"He gets along with everybody," Nagy said. "He talks to everybody. He's been a great teammate, and he's a great talent to be around. I'm excited to watch that up close."

One thing just in watching Shohei is you see that his talent is real."

—Mike Scioscia

CHAPTER 10

OHTANI CONTINUES TO BLOOM IN MAY

May 1

Shohei Ohtani returned to the lineup, and the Angels got back into the win column, snapping a four-game skid by beating the Baltimore Orioles, 3–2.

Ohtani, who missed two games with a sprained left ankle, rapped out a double that was noteworthy.

His seventh extra-base hit through 13 career games tied Jackie Warner (1966) for the most in franchise history.

What pleased Ohtani more was his team won, which isn't surprising for him.

The right-hander also wasn't taken off guard when the Angels skipped him in the rotation, as he didn't start the series opener because of a sprained left ankle. It's his left ankle, and foot, that absorbs the force of the 6-foot-4, 200-pounder's deliveries. So the Angels decided to push him back with his next start to be determined after a series of bullpen sessions.

May 2

It was an 0-for-4 night at the plate for Shohei Ohtani and a 1-for-1 night in collecting an award.

Ohtani's stunning start in the majors led to his winning the March/April American League Rookie of the Month Award from MLB.

Ohtani, who scored a run in the 10–7 win over the Baltimore Orioles, has starred as both a hitter and a pitcher since his debut on March 31.

He had four home runs and batted .341 with a .383 on-base percentage, and a 1.065 on-base-plus-slugging percentage.

In his four starts, he was effective in all but one, pitching to a 2–1 record with a 4.43 ERA. Over 20 1/2 innings, Ohtani had 26 strikeouts.

Not since Ohtani's pitching idol Yu Darvish in 2012 had a Japanese pitcher won the award.

"This is a great honor," Ohtani told Kyodo News. "Although I've only just begun, it's great to get off to a good start."

May 3

At first glance, it was Shohei Ohtani's solid night at the plate that would draw the attention of those tracking his rookie season.

But it was what happened before the game that had everyone in the Angels clubhouse talking.

Word came across that Seattle Mariners great and former Nippon Professional Baseball star Ichiro Suzuki was stepping away from his playing career.

The Mariners wouldn't use the word "retirement," as Ichiro, forty-four, wanted to leave open the possibility of playing next season.

But the timing of his announcement shattered the picture of Ichiro and Ohtani sharing a field. There was even chatter that Ohtani, who had his last start pushed back, would get the nod on Sunday in Seattle and possibly face Ichiro, which would be a monumental event in Japan.

But the showdown between the best player to ever come from Japan and one who hoped the same is said about him someday was not to be.

This passing of the torch would have to transpire outside the lines.

Since Ohtani signed with the Angels, and during spring training, baseball fans around the world had looked forward to these Japanese icons squaring off.

"I have nothing but the utmost respect for him," Ohtani said in a statement issued through the Angels. "What he has done for this game, our country, and the fans. I wish we could have played against him, but it wasn't meant to be. Wish nothing but the best for him moving forward."

Every baseball player in Japan looked up to Ichiro, and Ohtani was no different. Their biggest contrast was the stages of their careers in which they reached the majors.

Ichiro, who played for 17-plus years after nine seasons in Japan, arrived in the majors after establishing himself with the Orix Blue Wave. Ohtani, who was in NPB for five years, started his first MLB this season at age twenty-three.

It's easy to see why Ohtani would admire Ichiro so much. But the love for the All-Star outfielder wasn't restricted to Ohtani's locker. Throughout the Angels clubhouse, Ichiro was spoken about with reverence.

"I saw him in [2001] spring training and he was playing right field and you had heard so much about him," manager Mike Scioscia said. "It was like after four innings you go, 'Wow this guy is talented.'

"He had unbelievable range in right field, an unbelievable throwing arm, he could fly, and the way he did everything he was so fundamentally sound. He did so many things that he was a force in the major leagues for a long time.

"You used to stop to watch him whether he was running the bases, fielding, hitting. I think he could hit 15–20 home runs a year if he wanted to. He had that kind of power."

The secret? Albert Pujols, a three-time National League MVP, asked him after Ichiro reached first base once.

"Stretching," the limber Ichiro told the muscular Pujols.

"Then he says, 'I'm just really lucky.' I said, 'Yeah, 3,000-plus hits, you are that lucky. You really worked hard and earned every hit.' He was a fun guy to be around, with a lot of energy, and he was great for the game."

Few outfielders can match the Angels' Mike Trout in climbing fences and stealing homers from opponents. It was clear that Ichiro was on that very short list to rival Trout.

"It was definitely robbing home runs that he is pretty good at," Trout said. "I take pride in taking away hits and homers, and I'm sure he does, too."

Ichiro, a 10-time All-Star, made Pujols a victim with a defensive gem in the 2003 All-Star Game.

"It was when I had a chance to win the MVP, and only Ichiro, and maybe Trout, with their speed, make the play. Later on I said, 'Hey man, why you have to do it like that—it's an All-Star Game,'" Pujols said with a laugh.

It was no joke when someone mentioned to Trout, a two-time American League MVP, the number of hits Ichiro collected in his record-setting season of 2004.

"That is pretty crazy, 262," Trout said. "That is unbelievable and pretty impressive."

Pujols was asked about the hitting styles of Ichiro and Ohtani and if there are similarities.

"Coming from Japan, you look at those guys, and they have really good technique," he said. "I know they might have a lot of movement with their bat going forward, but the main thing as a player is that they keep their hands back and as a hitter that is a huge part of hitting, to keep your hands back and leave the bat back so long that you are able to get the ball deep in the strike zone and it was really unique.

"Ichiro was probably the first I saw do that. And when you see it you go, 'I don't know if that is going to work out,' but that guy was getting 200-plus hits a year."

Like Ohtani, both men excel in the running game.

"[Ichiro's] speed was unbelievable," Pujols said. "He would hit a two-hopper to shortstop, and he would beat it out."

May 4

Everyone knows it rains in Seattle. But a downpour of boos isn't such a common occurrence.

But that was what greeted Shohei Ohtani at every turn as he faced the Seattle Mariners at Safeco Field for the first time.

A safe bet in the offseason was Ohtani signing with the Mariners instead of the Angels. The Mariners have a great tradition with Japanese players, none better than with Ichiro Suzuki, and the organization met the criteria that Ohtani was seeking.

But despite all that and being on the West Coast as well, Ohtani headed for Southern California instead of the Great Northwest.

Or is that the Great Northboo?

Ohtani heard them with vengeance when approaching the plate leading off the second inning. Then when he struck out, one of the night's loudest cheers erupted.

"I'm not really used to being booed," Ohtani told mlb.com. "It was probably my first time, so it felt kind of awkward and a little weird."

But Ohtani didn't let the razzing bother him. He responded with two knocks, including a double, in raising his average to .339 as the Angels blanked Seattle, 5–0.

Albert Pujols also notched two hits, the 3,000th and 3,001st of his stellar career. He became the 32nd player to reach the 3,000-hit club and the second Dominican player after the Texas Rangers' Adrian Beltre.

Before the game, Ohtani met with Ichiro, with the younger Japanese star coming over to the Mariners' side of the field during batting practice. Ichiro's sense of humor was on display while he was mingling with others.

Just as Ohtani approached Ichiro's left shoulder and had removed his hat in his greeting, a cunning Ichiro sped off in the opposite direction. After five or six strides, Ichiro turned around and stopped, with an exuberant Ohtani matching his strides and removing his cap again. The pair exchanged a hearty handshake, with Ohtani bowing and Ichiro pointing back to his Mariners colleagues.

"When he signed with the Angels he did text me," Ichiro told mlb. com during spring training. "And obviously in the offseason I met with him a few times, obviously privately.

"He's mentally, definitely, tough. The [20-year] age difference, I am like a father and he is like a son. But mentally he's like a father and I'm like a son. So I think he is mentally tough."

Back to Ohtani being showered with the Bronx jeers on the West Coast. Scioscia smiled about it, maybe thinking of Hall of Famer Reggie Jackson's assertion that spectators don't boo nobodies.

"I think the Seattle fans were disappointed obviously that Shohei didn't sign here," Scioscia said. "It's almost a sign of respect. They wanted him and he obviously chose our club and we're thrilled that he did. He had good at-bats tonight."

May 6

It was a great day for Mariners fans, as they would have more time to razz Shohei Ohtani.

Restricted to giving Ohtani the business when he popped his head out of the dugout to bat in the opening game of the series, this contest was different. Ohtani was making his fifth pitching start in the majors, so the Seattle faithful, still upset that Ohtani didn't select the Mariners as his team, would have more time to voice their displeasure.

But really it was a pleasure to watch Ohtani work. This was a determined and dedicated craftsman going about his work in a stellar and charismatic fashion, which drew him a tip of the cap from the opposing manager.

"Ohtani threw the ball well," the Mariners' Scott Servais said. "The fastball has velocity. The secondary pitches are real—the curveball and slider and split-finger all have depth and are hard. Credit him. He got the job done today."

It came 12 days between starts, as his scheduled outing against the Baltimore Orioles on May 1 was scratched because of the sprained ankle he sustained while running out a grounder against the New York Yankees on April 27.

"I [felt] a lot more normal than I expected," Ohtani told mlb.com. "I felt like I was on normal days' rest."

Ohtani (3–1) worked into the seventh inning and allowed but two runs while striking out six giving him 32 on the year. By reaching the 30-strikeout standard in his first five career games, he joined Bo Belinksy (35, 1962) and Jered Weaver (31, 2006) as the only Angels to accomplish this feat.

"His stuff looked great," Scioscia said after Ohtani's 98-pitch performance.

And that made the Mariners fans' boos turn into boo-hoos. But Ohtani, in being polite, made a point to compliment the Mariners for being interested in his joining their squad.

"I want to pitch well against not just this team, but every other team that was pursuing me, to show them that they weren't wrong with their scouting," Ohtani said after surrendering just four singles in his first six innings.

Ryon Healy's two-run homer in the seventh ruined the shutout. His long fly came with a message that Ohtani absorbed, one of many in his historic rookie season.

"One big difference from Japan to here is everyone can hit home runs, from 1 to 9 [in the lineup], so I just need to stay sharp," he told the *Orange County Register*.

Once again, Ohtani proved the challenges in beating him. He has not one, but really four, effective pitches that he can basically throw any time in the count.

"All his pitches were working," catcher René Rivera said. "Not only his splitter, but the slider was nasty. The curveball was good. He mixed everything up to get those hitters off balance. He did a great job."

66

One big difference from Japan to here is everyone can hit home runs, from 1 to 9 [in the lineup], so I just need to stay sharp."

—Shohei Ohtani

Mariners fans did their best to get under Ohtani's skin over the weekend. But once again, he didn't blink. He left town avoiding a few arrows, and with a 3–1 record and a 4.10 ERA.

May 8

Shohei Ohtani's batting practices were worthy of getting on the sports shows' highlights reels in Japan. It's easy to see why as he regularly put on a display of unparalleled power in the hours before first pitch.

Ohtani has proven to be a can't-miss, must-watch player during the game. But if people could see him display his brawn during pregame, they would be even more amazed with this multitalented player.

He blasted several shots into the upper deck of Coors Field above right-center field, a part of the stadium where baseballs just don't land.

That's at mile-high elevation.

That's at sea level.

That's anywhere!

But with Ohtani in the cage and unable to start with no designated hitter in the National League ballpark, he abused one ball after another, many landing in The Rooftop Bar, where patrons aren't accustomed to fishing baseballs out of their schooners.

May 9

In a season of firsts, Shohei Ohtani added another one. Ohtani sprung off the bench in eighth inning of the Angels' 8–0 victory over the Colorado Rockies and got his first pinch hit. Because the Angels were playing in a National League ballpark, Ohtani's role as a designated hitter wasn't in play.

"Shohei has to get acclimated to that part of when he's available and when he can pinch hit," Scioscia told mlb.com. "It's good to see him get comfortable."

May 10

Watching Shohei Ohtani play is a kick. Watching him hit with one, not so much.

That's the observation as the two-way star has ceased lifting his right leg in an exaggerated manner to kick-start his swing.

Instead, he is rotating more on the tip of his right foot, after patting his bat on his shoulder, then extending it away from his body, and the results have been encouraging. He toe-tapped his way to his fifth home run as the Angels beat the Minnesota Twins, 7–4.

Once again, Ohtani's home run was far from a paint-scraper, easily surpassing the wall as the blast traveled 414 feet and left the bat at 108.7 mph.

In any league, that's one baseball that was scorched.

"It's not perfect yet, I'm still making adjustments every day, each at-bat," Ohtani told mlb.com. "Sometimes, it goes bad, so that's why I need to fix it. I don't feel like I've adjusted perfectly."

What he's also learning is the cat-and-mouse chase between pitcher and hitter. The early book on Ohtani was to bust him inside so he couldn't extend his powerful arms.

When that fails, the thinking is to attack him away and hope for soft contact off the end of the bat.

"I was still able to hit the [inside] ball pretty well, and hit for a good average, so maybe they're trying to test pitching me away," said Ohtani, who also added an RBI double.

"I still feel like they don't know how to pitch me, and I still feel the same way [back], so everything is still in progress."

Ohtani was just as impressive showing off his baserunning as his biceps. His hustle double on a ball hit to right-center was a blur of brilliance.

Running at a speed that nearly reached 20 mph, Ohtani touched second in 8.07 seconds from leaving home for the fastest Angels two-bagger this year.

Just one Angel bested that mark, and it was Ohtani when he covered that distance in 7.94 seconds en route to a triple.

He now has hit safely in 14 of his 16 starts as the designated hitter.

"We know he's dangerous," Twins manager Paul Molitor said. "Obviously, he's skilled offensively, and if he gets pitches, he's going to hit them."

May 18

The third-largest video board in the majors has a dent thanks to Shohei Ohtani.

The Angels' freaky-good rookie added to his legend before the Angels tangled with the Tampa Bay Rays by striking a ball in batting practice off the Angel Stadium video board in right-center field.

The sound of the ball departing his bat was what made everyone quickly turn and look. The necks craned into the sun bouncing off the right-field seats to see just where this epic blast would settle.

"The last time I saw a guy launch balls like that it was Barry Bonds," a National League scout said.

This shot blew past the 38 rows of seats and clanked against the 9,500-square-foot video board, above the numbers that have been retired in franchise history.

If Ohtani keeps shooting balls off his bat in this fashion, No. 17 might be hung up with the other six numbers someday.

For now, here's a digit to keep in mind: 513. That's how far Ohtani's shot was estimated to have traveled.

May 20

If it's Sunday, it must be Shohei Ohtani on the mound, and on this day, that meant the Minnesota Twins offense was on sabbatical.

Ohtani struck out a career-high 11 in the Angels' 2–1 triumph. He didn't pick up his fourth win despite being charged with but a run and three hits and two walks.

Sensational would be a good adjective to describe Ohtani's 6 1/3 innings of work.

"That was a pretty phenomenal start," Scioscia told the *Orange County Register*. "Not a solid start. That was phenomenal."

It caused players in both dugouts to shake their heads. Twins first baseman Logan Morrison mentioned Ohtani while alluding to a two-time American League MVP in Mike Trout.

"I think he's doing something that nobody has probably ever done, and it might be a long time before you see it again," Morrison said.

"There's another guy in that clubhouse who is a really good player, but to me, with what he does on the mound and with the bat, he's probably the best player in the world."

He is Shohei Ohtani.

"When he's on the mound, you forget that he's a hitter," Angels second baseman Ian Kinsler said. "You forget that he's our five-hole guy who can smash homers. When he's jogging around the bases after a home run, you forget that he's one of our best pitchers.

"It's a unique situation, and he's been extremely successful. It's fun to watch."

66

I think he's doing something that nobody has probably ever done, and it might be a long time before you see it again."

—Logan Morrison

Ohtani had just pitched one of his best games of his brief but meteoric career.

Previously known this season for reaching triple digits with his pitches (100 mph), he reached that plateau for the first time with his offerings (103).

Despite that heavy workload, among the first questions in the postgame press conference was one about his hitting.

Say what? In a Sunday game in which his bat took a rest, someone asked about his participation in the All-Star Game's Home Run Derby.

"It's an honor to be mentioned in that conversation," he told the *Orange County Register*. "But I still feel like I'm not at that level yet, so I need to keep showing up every day and putting up good results and we'll see from there."

But it was putting the Rays back on their dugout bench that Ohtani did with a flair in his seventh major-league start and his fifth being tabbed as "Sunday with Shohei."

"I think I can build from this outing to my next outing, build more trust and I can pitch longer," he said.

He's constructing, too, a reputation for being a player able to lift his game when the pressure increases.

"When people get on second base, he's a different animal," catcher Martin Maldonado said. "The fastball is different, the split finger is different, the slider is different. That's what impressed me."

Others were still consumed with Ohtani's jaw-dropping HR in BP two days earlier.

"There are just a handful of players you would pay for to go watch batting practice," a longtime National League scout said. "I saw Jose Canseco and Mark McGwire back in the 1980s, and in the 2000s it was Barry Bonds, Josh Hamilton, and Giancarlo Stanton.

"When I saw what Shohei could do, I was shocked. I just went, 'Whoa.' He belongs in that group of those players that you would pay for to see take BP."

May 25

Another city and another spurned fan base upset that Shohei Ohtani didn't join their team. The Yankees were all-in on Ohtani in the early stages. Then Ohtani decided he preferred a team on the West Coast, heading for Orange Couny instead of the Big Apple.

Ohtani would get but one at-bat in his Bronx debut, and it was far from a warm hand that greeted him. But that tidbit seemed insignificant when considering who Ohtani ended his evening against: flame-throwing reliever Aroldis Chapman.

New Yankee Stadium had an old-time feel when they faced each other in the eighth inning with the tying run in scoring position.

Ohtani got everyone's attention when he smoked a fastball down the left-field line foul, one that came in at 100.3 mph.

But Ohtani succumbed to Chapman with a ground ball to short, getting beat by a step as Yankees fans jumped to their feet.

"You could feel a little bit of electricity with those two," Yankees manager Aaron Boone told mlb.com. "Ohtani had some good swings on him, but Chappy was able to finish him off.

Ohtani, the star from the Far East, got a taste of East Coast baseball in playing before a vocal sellout crowd of 46,056. He was hitless in three at-bats, with a walk.

But no one was moving when Ohtani dug in and held his own against the lefty Chapman.

"It was a big situation," Ohtani said. "Obviously I really wanted to get a base hit, but I wasn't able to come through. All his pitches were really fast, really powerful. Some of the contact I made I thought was pretty good contact."

May 27

The day Japanese baseball fans had circled on the calendar ended up with a line through it, akin to the international sign of no-go.

The pitching showdown between former Japanese stars Masahiro Tanaka and Ohtani never materialized.

Ohtani was scratched from his start with the team being concerned about his workload.

Earlier in the week, the New York tabloids were in a tizzy about a Ohtani-Tanaka matchup, a headline declaring the game would be the "Center of the World."

"That would be pretty cool," Yankees manager Aaron Boone told the *New York Post*.

"Obviously, Ohtani has burst onto the scene as one of the talks of baseball with what he has been able to do on both sides of the ball. I'm sure if that happened it will be fun to be part of it."

NHK, as it does every time Ohtani pitches, telecast the game live in Japan at 2 a.m.

"The game will be watched all over the world," Yankees reliever Dellin Betances said.

But Ohtani still got to face Tanaka—as a hitter—for the first time in the majors.

Unfortunately for Ohtani, his first time wasn't a memorable one, as he struck out twice and drew a walk in three plate appearances against Tanaka in the Angels' 3–1 loss to the Yankees.

"He's a good pitcher," Ohtani told reporters. "I think he proved that today. But more than that, I'm upset that we lost."

The entire series was a lost cause not only for the Angels, but for Ohtani, who was booed by Yankees boosters still upset that he rebuffed New York's offer to join baseball's most famous team.

By the time the Angels had checked out of their Midtown Manhattan luxury hotel, Ohtani didn't have much to show for his visit: 0-for-9 with five strikeouts and four walks.

That Ohtani scuffled against Tanaka in New York was hardly news that was fit to print. When facing him in Japan in 2013, Ohtani was hitless in 11 at-bats that included six strikeouts. Of course, Ohtani was a teenager at the time.

"I don't think I'm putting too much pressure on myself any day, not even this time around," Ohtani said.

With his team struggling, and his average sinking to .291 on a road trip in which he went 3-for-19, Ohtani sought the sunny side of the street.

"I didn't get any hits this time, but I was able to draw some walks," he said. "I think that's a positive thing to take out of this series."

May 30

Shohei Ohtani was on the mound in the Motor City, revved to face the Detroit Tigers. But the weather insisted on this outing being anything other than a smooth ride.

After two rain delays, the second one lasting 41 minutes, Ohtani was lifted after throwing five innings and being charged with a run on three hits. Ohtani didn't get a decision in the Tigers' 6–1 victory over the Angels as he lowered his ERA to 3.18.

But he raised everyone's antennae when he fired a pitch 101.1 mph, the fastest by a starting pitching in the majors this season.

"It's just amazing how he's throwing 90, 91 and all of a sudden you see 98 out of nowhere when he really wanted to pump up," Tigers manager Rod Gardenhire told mlb.com.

Gardenhire, a baseball lifer, was impressed with the Angels rookie.

"A nice, big slow curveball, and really confident out on the mound," he said. "Yeah, that's a pretty nice-looking pitcher, a nice-looking young man who did really well."

With a really tricky splitter that disappears just before it's struck.

"As far as my hitting his splitter, I have no idea what I'm doing when I hit, man," Detroit right fielder Nicholas Castellanos said. "I just kind of look for something and swing hard."

Ohtani's splitter had turned into one of the most potent pitches in the majors. He entered his eighth career start after throwing 157 splitters this season and allowing just one hit. Batters are 1-for-44 when an Ohtani splitter is the final pitch they see in an at-bat. The swing-and-miss rate of 61 percent on his splitter is the second-best of any pitch in the majors.

"He has very powerful stuff," Castellanos said. "So I think when he comes to a place where he's harnessing that [slider] and he can play with 101 whenever he wants, that's kind of a Justin Verlander-type deal."

KINSLER FAMILIAR WITH DARVISH AND NOW OHTANI

Second baseman Ian Kinsler has seen a lot in his 13 years in the majors. Among the interesting aspects of his career is having a clubhouse seat in watching the arrivals of two Japanese stars: Yu Darvish and Shohei Ohtani.

Kinsler, who was traded to the Boston Red Sox, played with Darvish when he was with the Texas Rangers, and now he counts Ohtani as being among his former Japanese teammates.

While Darvish and Ohtani were from the same country, and the same Nippon Professional Baseball team, the Nippon-Ham Fighters, where they both wore No. 11, they weren't cut from the same mold.

"Not really," Kinsler said. "As far as in the fluidity in their bodies and mechanics, they are a little bit similar. But I think Darvish was [25] years old when he got here. I don't know if he was a finished product, but he definitely had more experience than Shohei.

"They were just different players, different mentality, different personalities. I think there are some similarities as far as the hype of them coming over from Japan and stuff like that."

Of course, Darvish was strictly a right-handed starter. Ohtani is trying to channel Babe Ruth while performing as a starter and hitting on a regular basis.

"Performing on both sides of the ball, I think, is insane," Kinsler said, leaning back in his chair and shaking his head in amazement. "You have to be extremely talented to do that at the major-league level; disciplined, prepared, schedule-oriented, and Shohei is really good about that. That is really special."

Kinsler knows of other players who excelled offensively and on the mound. But for one reason or another, they didn't attempt what Ohtani is trying in rewriting history and the way players are viewed.

"I think there are guys that get drafted that did both in college and they end up going one way or the other and then failing that way and then trying to go back to the other side and failing that way," Kinsler said. "It is very difficult to do and it really hasn't been done forever, or for a very, very long time when baseball was different."

Kinsler said he chuckled when those doubting Ohtani were vocal after he struggled during spring training. Once Kinsler saw him play, he wasn't concerned.

"The talent is incredible and the swing is extremely fluid and clean," he said. "And the way he runs, he is fluid. Same with the way he throws it 100 miles per hour.

"In spring training, just watching him and the way that his body moved, it was pretty apparent that this is a player that can do both. It's extremely unique, and I'm glad he's on our team.

"So far, so good, and hopefully he can continue for a really long time. I think that would be great."

CHAPTER 11

OHTANI'S ELBOW STALLS HIS HISTORIC JOURNEY

June 6

The Angels were taking on the Kansas City Royals in a routine, middle-of-the-week game. But with Shohei Ohtani set to make his ninth major-league pitching start, it was "Sho-Time" at Angel Stadium, and people were grasping at what that meant.

Ohtani starts are different, intriguing, and ones that spread far across and over the "Orange Curtain" of Orange County. Not only does Fox Sports West blanket Southern California with coverage, but NHK in Japan broadcasts the games to Ohtani's sleepy compatriots at 2 a.m.

Dedicated viewers ignore the early morning clock, never dreaming of missing their Ohtani-san.

Ohtani is an Angel, but he belongs to a much bigger universe than one wearing just bright red.

There's also the large Asian community in Southern California, especially Orange County, which hits pause on their routine when No. 17 is kicking mud off his cleats on the Angel Stadium mound.

71

Signs pop up all around the Big A in Japanese to give the "Big Shohei" more support. Every one of his pitches, it seems, is met with a cheer (on outs and strikes) and a noticeable groan (on base hits, walks, and balls).

How intriguing is Ohtani?

This day was a quirky one in Southern California in that someone could attend a doubleheader, with a single game at two stadiums.

The Padres played the Atlanta Braves in a matinee affair at Petco Park. With a fairly quick game, and a break or two with the traffic, reaching Angel Stadium to watch Ohtani that night wasn't a loony idea.

Some die-hard baseball fans accomplished it, a percentage of whom likely would have had little interest in doing so without the undeniable pull of watching Ohtani pitch.

"

Ohtani is an Angel, but he belongs to a much bigger universe than one wearing just bright red."

When he trotted to the hill to face the Royals, there was a different vibe to the crowd. People were watching him get loose and not so much their phones—if only to take a picture of baseball's emerging two-way star. Ohtani likely leads the majors in having his image preserved, and a quick check on Instagram shows the incredible number of times people point toward Ohtani and snap a shot.

But little did those focusing on him know that it might be Ohtani's last start of this season and of 2019.

Ohtani went to work against the lowly Royals, but his outing was cut short by a familiar ailment. After being charged with a run and four hits over four innings, Ohtani jogged back out for the fifth.

Catcher Martin Maldonado, who had immersed himself before the season in Ohtani videos to study his every move, felt something was askew. After Ohtani finished his warm-up tosses, Maldonado looked toward the dugout with an expression of alarm escaping from behind his mask.

Ohtani had nonchalantly completed his eight pitches before a batter was summoned, but Maldonado was hot on the trail of something disturbing.

"Normally he throws a lot of curveballs," Maldonado told mlb.com. "He threw a lot of fastballs when he was warming up, so I thought something was different with him."

Curse the blister, many thought, as this abbreviated appearance nearly matched his one against the Boston Red Sox on April 17. Same right hand, same middle finger, same spot of tender skin revolting from Ohtani's efforts.

Sure, Ohtani had struggled with his control in walking three leading up to the fifth.

Nonetheless, he struck out Abraham Almonte, the last batter he faced to end the fourth, and when strolling to the dugout afterward, he looked content and not the least bit concerned.

But the Angels looked at his finger and considered the future.

"You could see the beginnings of [a blister], and we obviously didn't want him to get past that," manager Mike Scioscia said.

Scioscia doesn't miss much, but even the veteran skipper was about to be surprised by the upcoming news regarding his standout right-hander. What began as an issue regarding a blister would blossom into the experienced manager fretting over a season-ending elbow injury to his star rookie.

June 8

The Angels were in the Twin Cities, and it was there that the second dose of bad news regarding Shohei Ohtani was disclosed.

After leaving his last start following four innings with the recurrence of blisters on his pitching hand, the Angels took a haymaker on the jaw.

Ohtani, while being tended to by the Angels training staff after his truncated start against the Kansas City Royals, informed those addressing his blister that his right elbow was stiff, too.

Further diagnosis and tests revealed Ohtani had suffered a Grade 2 strain of the right elbow's ulnar collateral ligament. Baseball observers know there is seldom good news that follows such a medical assessment.

Tommy John surgery is the ultimate course of action to repair frayed ligaments in many cases, a procedure that can cost a pitcher an estimated 12–14 months of his career.

It wasn't long after Ohtani signed with the Angels in December that Yahoo Sports reported his UCL had already suffered a Grade 1 sprain. That report said he underwent platelet-rich plasma and stem-cell injections to combat it.

With tests showing he now had a Grade 2 strain, it was clear that was the reason his elbow was tight. Ohtani wasn't trending in the proper direction.

A glum Mike Scioscia would now have to set his team's compass minus one of its biggest weapons.

"We're losing two significant parts of our club," the manager told the *Los Angeles Times*. "What he did on the mound to this point is really special. What he's done in the batter's box as a left-handed bat is very important to us."

It all seemed so cavalier when Ohtani exited early versus the Royals on June 6. Those dang blisters had become a nuisance again, but in the wake of that development, few leaped to the conclusion that Ohtani could possibly be out for the year with an elbow injury.

"It's a disappointment, but we just have to keep going," Scioscia said. "The schedule doesn't stop. We know he was doing a lot of special things for us, but you've got to move on."

Angels general manager Billy Eppler said if Ohtani weren't a pitcher, he could probably keep playing.

The Angels could assess the risk of Ohtani returning as a hitter, if the doctors allowed it, while putting his pitching career on hold.

Ohtani was a two-way phenom for the Angels, doing something that hasn't been done in nearly a century. The excitement he provided by his stellar play on both sides of the ball had created a buzz not only through the majors, but throughout the baseball world.

Over Ohtani's first 23 games, he went 4–1 with a 3.10 ERA and 61 strikeouts in 49 1/3 innings. He was batting .289 with six homers and 20 RBIs, as well.

But all didn't end well in his previous outing, and now Ohtani was headed to the disabled list, his rookie season absorbing a serious setback because of a strained elbow ligament.

June 22

It was a bullpen session in which most of the attention was focused 60 feet, six inches away from right-hander Felix Peña.

Shohei Ohtani, for the first time since landing on the disabled list with a sprained right elbow, was getting comfortable in a batter's box. Out in the Angels bullpen, Ohtani zeroed in on Peña's deliveries headed in his direction.

It's what's coming the Angels' way on June 28 that has them crossing their fingers. That's when the doctors will issue their report on the progress Ohtani's elbow has made after absorbing injections of platelet-rich plasma and stem cells.

It's possible Ohtani won't be cleared to return to any baseball activities. But there's also a chance he could return to hitting in the middle of the Angels order, even if his elbow is considered too compromised to begin pitching again.

There's no diagnosis yet that Ohtani needs Tommy John surgery, which is accompanied by roughly a 12–14-month recovery period.

So if Ohtani is required to have surgery, whether he undergoes it now or in the offseason, his pitching aspirations in 2019 would be for nil.

But if can return his skilled bat to the order, it's better than nothing. And since June 7, that's all the disappointed Angels had received from a mending Ohtani.

June 27

As the Angels await news on Shohei Ohtani's elbow, the prospects of his pitching again during his rookie season look dim.

Ohtani's ability to swing a bat? That outlook isn't nearly as dire.

Dr. Steve Yoon, a member of the Angels' medical staff, has told club executives that if it's determined Ohtani wouldn't do further damage to his mending elbow by swinging at pitches, he could return to the team's struggling lineup.

"I understand that he would clear him to be able to hit," Angels general manager Billy Eppler explained in an interview with MLB Network Radio. "If he says the ligament's in a good shape and has, in fact, scarred down."

Ohtani's right elbow was injected with platelet-rich plasma and stem cells on June 7 in a strategy to escape Tommy John surgery and accelerate healing in his sprained ulnar collateral ligament.

The Angels have lost four straight, and their offense is scuffling after scoring 10 runs in five games, a span in which they batted .185.

Ohtani has hit some potholes as well, with his average sinking to .289 from .342 thanks to an 8-for-41 skid over 13 games.

June 28

Since Shohei Ohtani was injured on June 6, the Angels have been grinding away, or chopping wood, a common phrase heard in clubhouses.

Now Ohtani can finally grab some wood after being cleared to resume hitting after getting the green light from the team's medical staff following his right elbow being reevaluated.

A fidgety Ohtani has gone from not swinging a bat to doing so one-handed, to tracking pitches in the bullpen, to getting the OK to take batting practice.

"To hear that he's allowed to take the next step toward rejoining our club as a hitter is news I wanted to hear," general manager Billy Eppler told the *Los Angeles Times*.

Just when manager Mike Scioscia can pencil in Ohtani's name on his lineup card will be determined.

"He'll let us know when he is ready," Scioscia said. "It could happen quickly. It could take a little more time. Whatever work he needs, we're going to make sure he doesn't skip any steps."

All true. Just like the Angels, and the legions of Ohtani fans, had a little more pep in their step knowing Ohtani was coming back.

MIKOLAS MADE THE SWITCH FROM MLB TO NPB AND BACK AGAIN

The challenges Shohei Ohtani faces in making the transition from Nippon Professional Baseball to the major leagues are considerable. It's something St. Louis Cardinals pitcher Miles Mikolas is well versed in, although in the opposite direction.

Mikolas is a key part of the Cardinals rotation, one season removed from plying his trade for the Yomiuri Giants. He understands what Ohtani is experiencing in being in a foreign country that speaks a language he doesn't have a firm grasp on.

All those things were true for Mikolas as he immersed himself in baseball, Japanese-style.

"Baseball is baseball, I feel like, once you get down to the nuts and bolts of it when you get in between the lines," Mikolas said before the Cardinals faced the San Diego Padres early in the season. "It's the same objective and the game is similar, but culturally, obviously, there's a lot of differences.

"There is an adjustment period where you accept most of it or you can kind of reject it. It is a learning experience in that aspect."

How so?

"Like workouts," the right-hander said. "They weren't big on weights and they like to spend a lot of time running. Now running has its time and place, but I didn't do as much running.

"And they throw a lot. I don't know of anyone that plays as much catch as Japanese pitchers. They have bullpens [sessions] every day and they are conditioned well for it. But over here, guys couldn't get away with it because they do them with so much effort."

In his three seasons with the Yomiuri Giants, Mikolas went 31–13 with a 2.18 ERA. He was open to explore ways the Japanese trained for baseball, although he admitted he embraced some techniques more than others.

"I said, 'Hey you know what, I'm in Japan and I'm going to try and do as many things their way as I can,'" said Mikolas, who pitched for the Texas Rangers and the San Diego Padres from 2012 to 2014. "If those things don't work out, or I don't like it, I go back to the things I know."

Mikolas recognized quickly that the Japanese aren't open to veering from what they believe is the right way in becoming a better player.

"They are very, very meticulous, very detail-oriented," he said. "They are not going to skip over steps and they would never take shortcuts. I would say I could do something this way that might be quicker or better, and they would say, 'No, no, no, we do it this way.'"

Mikolas, of course, couldn't have his grub his way. And that was among the biggest things he had to get accustomed to.

"Food and the language," he added.

That Ohtahi excelled in NPB gave some food for thought. If he could do it there, could he really do it in the majors, where the players are better and the season longer?

Through Mikolas's eyes, just how good is NPB?

"People describe it somewhere between Triple A and the big leagues, and that is pretty accurate," he said. "Guys are very, very talented and very, very polished.

"I think if their rules on free agency were different, you would see many, many more Japanese players in the major leagues. There is a fairly good amount of major-league–ready talent, or players that would need a very short adjustment period. But the Major League talent is over there, especially pitchers."

Where Mikolas noticed the biggest difference is how Japanese attack rivals offensively. It's more situational baseball than the majors' approach of nearly everyone from 1 to 9 in the order trying to launch home runs.

"There's a little more small ball, but there are infielders and outfielders that would be very good here," he said. "And there are guys with a lot of pop that could play the game here."

The reason Ohtani got here so quickly was that the Ham Fighters agreed to post him early, making him available to teams in the majors. That was part of the agreement the club had with Ohtani in coaxing him to play in NPB before he went to the majors.

"Their system is that's it's nine years before you can become a free agent, and if you enter the league at age 21 or 22, they are not able to leave until they are on the wrong side of 30," Mikolas said. "By then, they are too old to leave; they have families and they don't want to go.

"But there are a lot of guys over there, 24, 25, 26 that want to come play in the major leagues, but the teams will not allow them to leave. It's kind of tough and unfortunate. There are three, four guys on each team that are major-league–caliber players."

Ohtani proved in two months that he had the goods to compete against the world's best players. That he's done so both offensively and through his pitching isn't lost on Mikolas.

"He seems to be doing it pretty well right now," Mikolas said before Ohtani was diagnosed with a Grade 2 sprain of an elbow ligament. "It's a long season, longer than it is over there, and a lot of things are different. But the guy has tremendous talent, and it's fun to watch to see where it is going to go."

When Ohtani went from Japan to the majors, it seemed his legend grew considerably. Although he was a two-way player for the Ham Fighters, the hype around his game increased when he crossed the Pacific Ocean.

"Over there it didn't seem as big a deal that he was doing both, even though he was the only guy doing it, he was one of their superstars and he was always in the news," Mikolas said. "I guess it was because he had been doing it for a couple of years. I think it became a bigger deal when he came over here."

CHAPTER 12

OHTANI INCHES HIS WAY BACK TOWARD THE MOUND

July 3

The day before America celebrated its independence, Japan was toasting the comeback of Ohtani. Out since June 6 when landing on the disabled list with a sprained right elbow ligament, Ohtani was in uniform, although strictly as a designated hitter.

Ohtani, as well, was making his return to the Emerald City, a city that once never wanted him to leave.

He was nestled in the Angels lineup at Seattle, a place where he consistently received boos when Los Angeles made a visit in May. Still ticked that the West Coast team Ohtani picked to start his majors career was the Angels, and not the Mariners, Seattle fans remain sour.

Ohtani didn't have much choice through nine innings but to let those detractors jeer him and cheer the Mariners pitchers. Ohtani was hitless in four at-bats as the Angels fell to Seattle, 4–1.

In an unfortunate nod to the Fourth, Ohtani's performance was a dud.

He got blanked at the plate, with three of those appearances resulting in a U-turn to the dugout after getting punched out. Instead of notching swings and misses, he was producing them at the plate. The two simulated games "Sho-Time" played before a handful of curious observers weren't enough to mimic "The Show."

"It's a different atmosphere up here facing big-league pitchers in big-league stadiums," Ohtani told mlb.com. "I still need a little more time."

The Angels were out of sorts as well in a loss to the Mariners. Later, manager Mike Scioscia was out of patience for those concerned with Ohtani's hitting.

"Shohei just needs to see some pitches," he said. "He's going to be fine. His bat speed is there."

July 4

One day after failing to provide a spark, Shohei Ohtani ignited a fire under the Angels offense to help produce a 7–4 win and snap the surging Mariners' eight-game winning streak.

Ohtani advanced to first on catcher's interference in the second and sprinted all the way around on Luis Valbuena's double to left field.

Ohtani would score again on a Cole Calhoun single after Shohei collected the first hit in his comeback in the third. Before he was finished, he reached base three times, had two hits, and scored two runs.

"I was seeing the ball a lot better today compared to yesterday," Ohtani said to mlb.com. "So I felt like I took a pretty big step forward."

But it's different for Ohtani, as his detailed training regime incorporates pitching and hitting. He's off-kilter in not being able to pitch.

"Because my normal rhythm is batting while I'm also pitching, the other side of that is what I'm now doing feels unusual," Ohtani told Kyodo News.

July 6

Somewhere along Shohei Ohtani's unlikely journey from being a

Angels owner Arte Moreno and Shohei Ohtani greet the crowd at Angel Stadium in December, 2017, as the two-way star is introduced to Angels fans.

(Left) Wearing his bright red No. 17 Angels jersey for the first time, the Japanese star tips his hat to admirers at his press conference at Angel Stadium. Ohtani picked the Angels out of seven finalists, citing his "connection" with the team.

(Above, right) Spring training arrives and so do Shohei Ohtani and his interpreter, Ippei Mizuhara. Ohtani was overmatched during the exhibitions games, at the plate and on the mound. With a .125 batting average and a 27.00 ERA, Ohtani, some naysayers suggested, would be better off opening the season in the minor leagues. *Courtesy of the Los Angeles Angels*

It's all smiles at Tempe Diablo Stadium as Shohei Ohtani, with his interpreter Ippei Mizuhara close behind, meets with Angels manager Mike Scioscia before the team starts its spring training workouts.

Ohtani diligently works on his pitching motion in spring training as he gets accustomed to his new team in a new league in a new country. It was a rough spring for Ohtani as he concentrated on his mechanics while others focused on his uneven performances.

Few players are more limber than Ohtani, and here he is going through his pre-workout stretching routine with other members of the Angels staff.

Ohtani's dream of reaching the majors finally comes true as he makes his debut at Oakland on March 29, 2018. In his four at-bats against the Athletics, Ohtani produces a single, which elicits a high five from first base coach Alfredo Griffin.

Mike Trout and Ohtani formed an early bond in spring training and it carried over into the season. Trout congratulates Ohtani after he collected his first major-league hit.

Ohtani fights off an outside offering against the Oakland Athletics as rival hurlers try to determine how to pitch to the left-handed slugger. Initially, Ohtani had to prove he could handle the inside pitches before pitchers changed their tactics.

(Right) Watching the fluid, athletic Ohtani pitch is almost like watching a ballerina, as each step and motion is a choreographed maneuver to get his body in the best possible position to deliver a strike. Ohtani won his second straight start and his debut in Anaheim by taking a perfect game into the seventh inning against the Athletics on April 8.

(Left) Shohei Ohtani shines in his win over the Oakland Athletics in his first start at Angel Stadium. Ohtani took a perfect game into the seventh inning, with the sold-out crowd cheering wildly on every pitch. Ohtani lifted his record to 2-0 by striking out 12 over seven scoreless innings. Ohtani was the first player since 1919 to win twice and hit three home runs in his team's first 10 games. *Courtesy of the Los Angeles Angels*

(Right) "Sundays with Shohei" became a must-see weekend event around Major League Baseball as fans flocked to ballparks to watch the two-way phenom take the mound. With Shohei Ohtani pitching just once a week, six of his 10 starts came on Sundays. *Courtesy of the Los Angeles Angels*

(Left) Ohtani gets the water cooler treatment after appearing on the post-game show following a dominating start against the Athletics, his first home start. Ohtani quickly proved, after a string of shaky spring performances, that he belongs in the majors.

(Left) Shohei Ohtani's home debut with the Angels comes with a bang as he hits his first home run in the majors. Ohtani crushed a three-run blast off Josh Tomlin to become the first player to earn a win in one game, then homer as a non-pitcher in his next game, since Babe Ruth in 1921.

(Right) After his teammates gave Shohei Ohtani the cold shoulder when he returned to the dugout after his first home run, a joyous celebration couldn't be delayed too long. The reactions by Ohtani's teammates reveal he is quickly becoming one of the team's most popular players.

Shohei Ohtani has a welcoming committee awaiting, with Andrelton Simmons and Sherman Johnson eager to greet him at home plate. In his first three games at Anaheim, Ohtani had six hits, three home runs, and seven RBIs.

While icing his shoulder following a start, Shohei Ohtani chats with the pool of international reporters following the Angels. Games in which Ohtani pitches are shown on TV live in Japan, as the country thirsts for any news regarding its favorite two-way phenom.

Two Japanese stars square off against each other as the New York Yankees' Masahiro Tanaka works the strike zone's bottom half against Ohtani. Tanaka, who held Ohtani hitless in 11 at-bats when they played in Japan, got the better of him this day with Ohtani going 0-for-2, with a walk.

It's a crowded mound as Angels manager Mike Scioscia checks in on Shohei Ohtani, along with the Angels trainer and Ippei Mizuhara, Ohtani's interpreter, during a June 6 game. Ohtani was removed from the game because of the recurrence of blisters, but later it was learned he sustained a sprained elbow ligament.

It's high fives all around after Shohei Ohtani sends another pitch over the fence. Ohtani's at-bats create a buzz at Angel Stadium, and on the road, as fans marvel at his skills and the joy in which he plays the game.

Shohei Ohtani celebrates another homer with another rookie, teammate David Fletcher. Ohtani would go on to become the second Japanese player to hit at least 20 home runs, joining former New York Yankee Hideki Matsui. Ohtani considered Matsui his hitting idol when growing up.

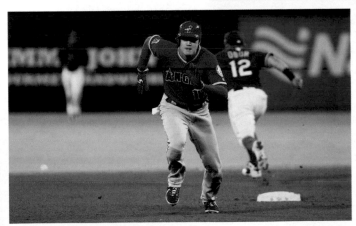

Shohei Ohtani is among the fastest Angels and he proves it when picking up an extra base against the Texas Rangers after an errant throw to second. Ohtani's speed is a big part of his considerable talents, as his times to first and second base this season were among the fastest on the club.

The Angels' two stars became fast friends after Mike Trout helped recruit Ohtani in the offseason. Trout often treats Ohtani like a younger brother by teasing Ohtani. With them hitting back-to-back later in the season, some Angels fans started calling the middle part of the order, "Troutani."

Shohei Ohtani makes the turn at first base after blasting home run No. 21 of his rookie season. Ohtani's first-inning shot off Adrian Sampson of the Texas Rangers exploded from his bat at 112.9 mph, making the 428-foot homer the hardest one hit by Ohtani this year.

Japan's Shohei Ohtani doesn't temper his emotions after striking out the USA's Mike Trout, a three-time AL MVP, to give Japan a 3–2 victory and its third World Baseball Classic title in March 2023. The two Los Angeles Angels teammates provided a game-ending at-bat that will go down in baseball lore. *Getty Images*

Japanese high school star to having a starring role in his Freeway Series debut against the Los Angeles Dodgers, he learned about baseball's ultimate test: to play every out, to fight on every strike until the game was determined.

But in the ninth inning, the outcome was a forgone conclusion, to many, when the Dodgers' All-Star closer, Kenley Jansen, held a 2–1 edge and the Angels by their collective throats.

Soon a long, hot day in Anaheim that included the warmest first-pitch temperature (108 degrees) in franchise history would be put on ice.

The Angels' 27 offensive outs had dwindled to one when Ohtani strolled to the plate, with his club down by one run. Once Shohei was in the batter's box, Jansen raced to an 0-2 advantage.

That's when Ohtani's discerning eye dominated, as he declined to nibble at Jansen's borderline pitches in drawing a walk.

From being down to their final strike, the Angels saw Ohtani galloping down the first base line as Jansen lamented his inability to finish off Ohtani and the Angels for the triumph.

Aboard as the tying run, Ohtani took off to steal second base and get in scoring position. He tested catcher Yasmani Grandal's right arm and swiped a bag that came with a bonus.

As Grandal's high throw sailed away, Ohtani was up, up, and away to third, the benefactor of the bumbling Dodgers' third error.

When teammate David Fletcher provided a single, Ohtani scored the game-tying run. It was followed by Ian Kinsler's game-winning hit to cap quite a Freeway Series introduction to Ohtani, and the extra satisfaction that accompanies beating the Dodgers.

A charmed life for Ohtani after surviving an 0-2 hole to Jansen. Maybe so. But so what, as Ohtani proved in yet another way, with his batting eye, he could contribute to an Angels win.

With him unable to pitch in by pitching because of his mending elbow, at least Ohtani had his potent bat. But against countryman Kenta Maeda, Ohtani's lumber was in a slumber.

Ohtani struck out in his first at-bat and sent a harmless popup into the air in his second go-around, his career showing against Maeda diving to 2-for-9.

"But I still wanted to get on base and help the team come back and win," Ohtani told mlb.com.

The game also revealed Ohtani's resolve, as he neglected to wave a white flag when all looked lost for the Angels against the intimidating Jansen.

"I think we just showed them that we're never going to give up," Ohtani said, "until the last out."

The Dodgers never did get that last out, and for the first time, Ohtani had pried opened his considerable set of tools and unveiled his baserunning ability to tie a game. After checking off the boxes of doing just that with his arm and his bat, he added his athletic body's lower half by heisting a key bag.

"He definitely has the technique and speed to steal a base when it's important," Scioscia told the *Los Angeles Times*. "And it's not always how many you're stealing. If you're stealing them at the right time, you can influence the game like he did [Friday] night."

It was a night of stars, and it was the Angels' newest one that provided the dramatics that were perfect for a Hollywood script.

But when the spotlight found Ohtani, it was his swift legs, and not his rocket-like right arm or poetic left-handed swing, that was the difference.

Run, Shohei, run, and when he did, he helped lift the Angels to another victory.

July 10

The Mariners made the Angels sweat a bit, but Los Angeles held on for 9–3 win. It was another night in which Shohei Ohtani contributed, with a sure-fire RBI single and a chopper to second baseman Dee Gordon that resulted in an error. Ohtani's speed, which forced the errant throw, showed again that there are few players in the majors in the Japanese star's class for quickness.

On his hit to left-center, Ohtani took a 94.4 mph fastball that was lingering on the outside corner at the top of the zone. Ohtani let his bat travel to where the ball was pitched, shooting it to the grass on a 104.5-mph line drive.

Everyone knows Ohtani can hit. Not as many realize that he's among the fastest players on the Angels and is there no end to his talents.

Gordon, a speedster himself, recognized how quickly and smartly Ohtani left the batter's box once his ground ball sprung in his direction. The second baseman got to it cleanly, but his toss was awry as Dee rushed his relay.

The jets were on as Ohtani ran at 29.6 feet per second. Scouts note that 30-plus is the elite territory for players. Overall, it took Ohtani four seconds to travel from home to first.

When the Angels squeezed the last hope out of the Mariners, it was time for the rocks in center field to be illuminated by the fireworks and the halo that tops the Big A to flash, signaling to Orange County that the Angels had prevailed.

The Angels, as is their custom, lined up for the postgame high fives, one of the perks of scoring more runs than a rival. The walk to the middle of the infield for the players coming from the bench traveled over the mound as they rushed to salute their victorious teammates.

It was an odd route for Ohtani, and it was clear to see his mind was wandering as the haze from the fireworks hung around, much like Angels fans happy with a win over the Mariners in the race for a potential American League wild-card berth.

As Ohtani started to climb the incline of the mound, he revealed where his heart was on a night that he was restricted to being the designated hitter.

For a moment Ohtani stalled, lingering over the rubber and lovingly touching it with his foot as if only his damaged elbow would allow him to pitch and be the two-way player he dreamt of. But those plans were on hold, a development that possibly had a hold on Ohtani's thoughts as his foot left its mark on the rubber and fell back in line.

The high fives came next, but the one from Ohtani's catcher, Martin Maldonado, was different. It came with a playful punch in Ohtani's chops, which did nothing to knock the smile of his onetime battery-mate's face after another win.

July 16–19

The All-Star Game has arrived and with it came four days off for Ohtani. That's a far cry from May, when Ohtani was being mentioned not only as a likely candidate to play in the game as a pitcher or a hitter, but also to participate in the Home Run Derby.

But a sprained elbow ligament shot down those hopes as Ohtani missed about a month of action. While he's returned to his designated hitter role, Ohtani has yet to pitch again.

Still, it was an electrifying first half, with Ohtani quickly showing fans of the major leagues what their counterparts in Nippon Professional Baseball knew long ago: Ohtani is a star, and a unique one at that.

His batting showed a slash line of .283/.365/.522, and it came with seven home runs and 22 RBIs.

As a pitcher, he worked 49 1/3 innings, compiling a 4–1 record with a 3.10 ERA. He struck out 61, while walking 20.

That's far from a pedestrian performance for any rookie, but especially one arriving with the hype that accompanied Ohtani.

"I didn't set any expectations for myself before the season," he told mlb.com. "I just wanted to see how things panned out. I had to get through some ups and downs, but overall it went pretty well."

Manager Mike Scioscia isn't one to offer faint praise. But he can't hide how impressed he is with Ohtani.

"Shohei has shown that his talent is real, and he can play at a very high level in the major leagues," the skipper said. "We're excited about that. I think he's done remarkably well for a young player coming over with so much on his plate."

Ohtani has looked more at ease batting against right-handers, which is why he seldom starts against southpaws. Ohtani has a .508 on-base-plus-slugging percentage when facing lefties, which pales to his 1.032 OPS versus righties.

"I've been saying this the whole time, I don't really feel uncomfortable hitting lefties," Ohtani said. "I hit them pretty well in Japan, so I just prepare myself for every at-bat. Of course, if I have better results, there are better chances I'll be starting against lefties. But ultimately that's up to Mike Scioscia, so I don't have much to say in it."

But he does have a say in the Angels' chances of winning. Over the first half with Ohtani in the lineup in some capacity, the Angels were 31–21 and 18–27 if he didn't pitch or hit. When appearing as a pinch-hitter, the Angels split 10 games.

Maeda, a former pitching star in Japan like Ohtani, isn't divided about his compatriot's first half: "I think he did very well as a hitter and a pitcher. I think what he is doing is extremely challenging."

Maeda noted that Ohtani's early success as a two-way player is a source of pride at home.

"By representing Japan, I think the Japanese people are happy that he is succeeding in doing something different," Maeda said. "And, yeah, I think it is very astounding that he is able to do both, considering the level of play here is a lot higher."

Ohtani wasn't at the All-Star Game in Washington, DC, but he was spotted over the break where the stars hang out. Wearing a fitted white T-shirt with a black cap and toting a backpack—looking pretty much like any other 20-something-year-old on holiday—Ohtani visited Universal Studios in Hollywood.

July 20

Ohtani the pitcher was back. Well kind-of, sort-of, maybe.

While the Angels readied for a three-game showdown with the defending world champion Houston Astros, Ohtani showed no problems tossing the ball around with his interpreter, Ippei Mizuhara.

The Angels' two-way sensation was letting a ball gingerly roll off his fingertips. Ohtani wasn't popping the glove. But his plopping something other than an imaginary ball toward somewhere else was the start on his road back to the mound.

One day after being cleared by the club's doctors, Ohtani began a throwing program. The endgame is hopefully having him pitch in a game before the season ends, with the platelet-rich plasma and stem-cell injections healing his elbow in a manner that might avoid Tommy John surgery.

So the first step was just that as the Angels brass got set to proceed with caution and optimism.

"We do anticipate him pitching for us this year if everything with his rehab goes as planned," Scioscia said in English before it was translated into Japanese.

Billy Eppler, the team's general manager, was also upbeat when updating reporters.

"We just need to do what's best for the player," Eppler told ESPN. "If it lends itself to him making starts here, great. If it takes longer, then it takes longer. We just have to stay flexible."

The Angels have learned to bend their ways to accommodate Ohtani. That dates to the offseason presentation they made to Ohtani to join the Angels, and they certainly weren't going to get stubborn considering his return to pitching.

Among the distinctive things about Ohtani is how the Angels are forced to consider new ideas when dealing with a hitter and a pitcher. For almost every instance in baseball, there is a set road map in the rehabilitation process to consider any and all challenges.

But with Ohtani's arsenal of skills being so extraordinary, much of what the Angels use as a template is written in pencil, not ink.

"He's a unique player with unique demands on him physically that go above and beyond a regular pitcher and go above and beyond a regular hitter," Eppler said. "I think it's just important to be mindful that he's going to take these steps of his throwing progression step by step."

With Ohtani's return, though, came a return of the doubters. Those who often scoffed at the team for thinking a player could handle the challenges as a pitcher and a hitter smirked. To consider that the Angels and Ohtani could avoid elbow surgery through a non-invasive treatment seemed like a long shot.

Then again, Eppler repeated to various media outlets that not one doctor hanging their shingle at the Kerlan-Jobe Orthopedic Clinic had suggested a surgical procedure that requires a 12- to 14-month rehabilitation window.

"

He's a unique player with unique demands on him physically that go above and beyond a regular pitcher and go above and beyond a regular hitter."

—Billy Eppler

"I can tell you the consensus among that group is to never push a player into surgery," Eppler said. "I gotta take the advice of the people that spend a lot of time and a whole lot of money getting those degrees."

Mike Scioscia has the equivalent of a Master's in baseball considering his 13-year playing career and his 19 seasons at the Angels' helm. While he's upbeat about Ohtani throwing again, he told everyone not to get overly excited.

"This is like Stage 1 where they got to get to Stage 10," he told the *Los Angeles Times*. "This is not a challenging period that he is in."

That will come, Scioscia promised, if Ohtani advanced minus setbacks.

"I would suggest just relax and enjoy the fact that he's throwing and stay tuned to when it gets really exciting," Scioscia said.

While all pregame signs were encouraging with Ohtani throwing a baseball and producing a spirited batting practice, it wasn't rainbows and unicorns when the game started.

The Astros, the defending world champions, had southpaw Dallas Keuchel on the mound. Keuchel is a former Cy Young Award winner, and Ohtani's Achilles' heel this season is hitting lefties.

No Angel from either side had much success against the crafty Keuchel, whose thick, dark, menacing beard is among his distinguishing features.

The Angels didn't get a hit until there were two outs in the seventh inning, and Ohtani had nothing to show for his evening in Orange County. His three at-bats produced three strikeouts.

But the game was secondary news to how the afternoon started with Ohtani playing catch with his interpreter, and seeing him throw again brought smiles to Angels coaches and players.

The tosses weren't very far, and Ohtani certainly wasn't putting much zip on the ball. It was, after all, Mizuhara receiving the most anticipated deliveries in Anaheim in some time.

Getting the green light to throw again after six weeks was significant. There's no way to tell if Ohtani, with his 4–1 record at the time, will pitch again this season. There's still a chance he will hit roadblocks en route to building back up one of the most talked-about right arms in the majors this season.

Then again, Ohtani has proved so many so wrong to date. Many decline to bet against him and his quest to resume his career as a starter.

"There is a template, but it is tough to fill in all the details until you see how all the details go," Scioscia said. "You have to be flexible. But we do anticipate him pitching for us this year if everything in his rehab goes as planned.

"I just think it is important to be mindful that he is going to take these steps in his throwing progression, and if he is feeling good, the distances will be increased and the time of the throwing progression will increase. But I can't answer the question of when he would potentially be back on the mound in a major-league baseball game."

Scioscia said Ohtani's valuable right arm will tell them when to proceed and when to retreat.

"We just need to do what is best for the player, and if it lends itself to making starts here, then great," he said. "And if it takes longer, it takes longer. We have to be flexible with it and how he hits every step of this progression."

July 23

The Angels reached the 50–50 mark, but it was hardly a jackpot they were splitting. Instead, it was their record after 100 games, as a season that bolted from the gate with such promise was showing signs of running out of gas.

Ohtani, though, slugged his eighth home run, and this one to dead center field was a big hit in Japan even in a 5–3 loss to the Chicago White Sox. Since earlier in the month, Ohtani's long flies have caused a look-alike puppet to pop from a Japanese news anchor's desk. The puppet not only has an uncanny resemblance to Ohtani, but his swing is almost a carbon copy of the left-handed rookie.

So after Ohtani rifled a 435-foot blast, someone in Japan was eager to cue the Ohtani puppet!

But it was the Ohtani that didn't have any strings attached that caused the White Sox concern.

"We'll, he's got some power," White Sox manager Rick Renteria told mlb.com. "The first ball he hit, his first at-bat, he flew out deep, right? We looked at one another and went, 'OK, this kid has power.' Then he put one in the turf in center field, and we said, 'Confirmed.' Good-looking young player."

July 25

It was "Big Game James" versus "Sho-Time" and which player with a cool nickname would back down first.

The lethargic Angels, losers in five of their past six games, were in need of a boost, so manager Mike Scioscia juggled his lineup. He elevated Ohtani into the lineup's No. 2 hole as the Angels faced veteran right-hander James Shields.

"We've been talking about this possibility for a week," Scioscia told the *Los Angeles Times* in his pregame media scrum. "I think the timing is right now to make the change."

Ohtani switched a close game into a rout when he took Shields deep in the fifth inning for a home run. His ninth on the season was a rocket and propelled 446 feet. It was Ohtani's second-longest shot since his 449-foot blast in April.

There was little doubt Ohtani squared up Shields's offering. Just like there was no question what it meant to Angels starter Tyler Skaggs.

Once Ohtani's crushed baseball finally landed, the TV cameras focused on Skaggs. He was dancing about in the dugout and wearing a grin as if privy to that night's lottery numbers.

"I like to show my emotions," Skaggs said. "Maybe not like that. But I was pretty excited."

July 29

It's before the game on a sun-splashed and downright hot Sunday afternoon. Before the Angel Stadium gates swung open, Ohtani was taking the field clutching his glove for a right-handed pitcher and not the bat he swings left-handed.

Seldom does a game of catch seem to carry so much weight with the Angels' media contingent, including more than 20 Japanese members, as they click away at his every toss.

On this day, Ohtani isn't tossing the ball to his interpreter Ippei Mizuhara, but a teammate. Ohtani isn't casually tossing the ball back and forth like other position players do when getting loose, instead supplying some zip to his relays.

Instead, Ohtani was in his pitching motion, ever so slowly, ever so exact, with each move from his languid, athletic frame looking to be a well-thought-out maneuver. Ohtani, far from the spectators' eyes, was inching his way back to throwing with his full force. But he did so with a calmness about him, although some could argue it was apprehension, as he knew one wrong tug at his mending ulnar elbow ligament could end his dream of pitching again this season.

To some, this session of long toss doesn't look like much. But to those studying Ohtani's carefulness with each step and his precise process in his flowing delivery, something else was in play. He was now at about 110 feet in distance, which is telling, as each ball left his hand cleanly with no wasted motions.

IN ANY LANGUAGE, McNAMEE IS AMONG THE ANGELS' MVPS

There's no denying Shohei Ohtani's popularity with Angels fans.

When he strolls to the plate at Angel Stadium after his name is announced, his cheers are often louder than those directed toward Mike Trout or Albert Pujols.

When Ohtani climbs the mound as the starter, there is a real buzz in the crowd.

But those tracking his every move aren't restricted to the American press. Not only do roughly 20 Japanese reporters chronicle him on a daily basis, there's a handful of media types from South Korea, China, and Taiwan, too.

That's a lot of mouths to feed for translated quotes. While Ippei Mizuhara is Ohtani's interpreter and constant companion, the press leans on Grace McNamee for their verbal nuggets from manager Mike Scioscia and others regarding Ohtani, the Angels' intriguing two-way star.

"My main role is to keep open the line of communication between the team and the international media that cover us," McNamee said. "I make sure they have everything they need."

The Angels have a seasoned pro in McNamee. Coming on the heels of Ohtani's signing in December, she contacted Tim Mead, the Angels' vice president of communications, to see if the club needed assistance with its exciting new import.

"I wanted to get back into baseball," she said. "I thought this would be a great opportunity if we could work something out."

McNamee, a Japanese-American who is fully of Japanese descent, had already earned her stripes as a translator. She worked with former Japanese star Hideo Nomo when he was with the Los Angeles Dodgers, along with his translator, Michael Okumura, so the fit with the Angels for this Orange County resident seemed perfect.

While manager Mike Scioscia's Japanese is far from perfect, he does attempt to speak in short spurts with McNamee and the foreign reporters. They banter and joke about how successful he is, while always appreciating the effort he puts forth.

However, there's no kidding around when McNamee is holding court. When a media member attempted a follow-up question before McNamee could translate a Scioscia comment into Japanese, he blocked the inquiry like he once did home plate for the Dodgers.

"Hey, wait a minute," he chided a reporter. "Don't step on Grace."

McNamee's first name is appropriate, as she provides a calming vibe to the chaos that can mark Scioscia's media sessions whenever Ohtani is the topic—which is just about every day.

Scioscia handles the language barrier with ease. Not only was he with the Dodgers when Nomo arrived, but he saw firsthand Fernando Mania, the hoopla that accompanied Mexican starter Fernando Valenzuela when he burst onto the scene in Los Angeles.

"Mike is very multilingual, and you see him speaking Spanish to some players in the clubhouse and trying to learn Japanese," McNamee said. "That is just the thing that makes Mike who he is. He has been great with the Japanese media, and they can relate to him. He puts them at ease.

"I think Mike does a great job in getting his players and others to feel comfortable around him, and I feel like breaking down the language barrier by learning words in Spanish and Japanese is one of those things. In my experience, people feel comfortable when they see you make an effort in trying to understand their language and culutre."

Why does Ohtani have Japanese fans so worked up, as they thirst for information on his every at-bat, outing, or even a spoken word or two?

"We had one of his former coaches from the Ham Fighters here with a TV crew, and he had mentioned that Shohei is like everybody's kid in Japan," McNamee said. "They all cheer for him and want him to succeed."

McNamee points to Ohtani's unique baseball skills as the main reason fans flock to him like a moth to a light bulb. But there's more in play than his play, according to McNamee.

"He's the whole package and a very well-liked person," she said. "In talking to a couple of his [Japanese] coaches, he's just a great person. I think it goes to his personality. He is very humble, respectful, focused, and he really works hard."

Finding anyone of Japanese descent not rooting for Ohtani would be really difficult. Count McNamee as among those enjoying Ohtani's historic ride into the record books as he performs feats not done in the majors in a century.

"I am very proud of him and I think anybody would be," McNamee said. "It's like when you see somebody that works so hard and is trying to continuously challenge themselves to become better, you just want them to succeed. For him to put up those numbers he has been able to, it makes all of us very proud.

"I just think that anybody who sees—he's not the underdog—someone try so hard and putting in lot of effort, whether that's sports, academics, whatever it is, you want to see that person rewarded with success. You respect that effort and I think that is the case with Shohei. He is a very easy guy to root for."

That's true in any language.

CHAPTER 13

OHTANI ENTERS AUGUST LOOKING TO GET RIGHT AGAINST LEFTIES

THE DOG DAYS of August are here, and Ohtani has more bark than bite when hitting left-handed pitchers. Like for any player, pitchers find holes in swings. It's up to the hitter to adjust, and the left-handed hitting Ohtani is doing just that.

But that doesn't mean the learning experience isn't long and challenging. Ohtani seldom fails, but when facing southpaws, it hasn't always gone right.

Ohtani entered August hitting .170 (9-for-53) with a .400 on-base-plus-slugging percentage, zero homers, and two RBIs, with 22 strikeouts, when digging in against lefties.

Compared that with a .296 average and a .967 OPS, with nine homers, 23 RBIs, and 34 strikeouts against righties.

Angels hitting coach Eric Hinske was straight about what has gone wrong: curveballs from lefties to lefties aren't easy to make contact with. That's especially true with Ohtani's tendency to lean out of his swing against a southpaw.

"We're just trying to keep him in there, you know," Hinske told Mike DiGiovanna of the *Los Angeles Times*. "He has a tendency to want to fall out of it and have that sort of Ichiro-like swing leaning toward first base. We're trying to keep him over the plate so he can go opposite field with that pitch."

Throw it straight and fast, no matter the arm a pitcher uses, and Ohtani can give it a whack. He did just that when Tampa Bay Rays lefty Jose Alvarado tried to sneak a 95-mph fastball by him, and it ended up being smoked to center for a single.

Hinske, a former major leaguer, is confident Ohtani will handle southpaws better as he learns the pitchers and gets more chances to conquer them.

"I definitely think he will continue to improve," Hinske said. "The ceiling with Shohei is endless."

While Ohtani has dazzled millions of fans with his greatness and uniqueness, it's easy to forget his earning his baseball stripes. His baby face comes with someone in the infant stages of playing in the majors.

"He's still a rookie, he's new to the league, seeing these guys for the first time," Hinske said. "And hitting in the big leagues is pretty tough."

So is Ohtani, and he'll attack this aspect of his game as he does every other one. With an unrelenting resolve to be the best he can be.

August 4

Cleveland has the Browns' Dawg Pound, the Rock & Roll Hall of Fame, and, at one time, NBA star LeBron James. Soon after James left for the Los Angeles Lakers, Ohtani showed the Buckeye State what all the commotion was about regarding his season.

Ohtani was dazzling in the Angels' 7–4 win over the Indians. He went a career-best 4-for-5 with two home runs and three RBIs, including a key single in the eighth off southpaw Oliver Pérez, which fueled a rally that helped snap the Angels' four-game losing streak.

"That's what Shohei can do, that's his talent," manager Mike Scioscia told mlb.com.

That his last hit came against a lefty didn't go unnoticed. Except maybe by Ohtani.

"I'm not trying to think about it too much, about righty-lefty, but I've been having better at-bats against righties and lefties," Ohtani told mlb.com. "The ball has been going in the right direction, and I'm starting to feel more comfortable."

He was at ease early, stroking a two-run homer off Mike Clevinger in the first inning. His 10th long fly was his first one on the road, as he redirected the right-hander's 96-mph fastball over the left-field fence.

Clevinger was a victim again in the third, as Ohtani unloaded a massive 443-foot blast to tie the game.

"Both pitches were pretty poorly executed," Clevinger said. "I mean, he's got tremendous power—don't get me wrong. The first [home run] was inside and he still put it the other way, so that's pretty impressive."

Despite the Indians being among the American League's top teams, Ohtani has abused the Tribe's pitching staff. His four home runs against them is the most he's hit against any team. The second one that nearly went 450 feet caused a head shake or two.

"Our jaw dropped on that one, but we see Shohei hit the ball hard," said Scioscia, an old-school former catcher who doesn't distribute hyperbole on a regular basis. "It was a long way, but the one in left field was the most impressive, because it's tough to get it out to that part of the park.

"It's almost like the Green Monster out there, but it's normal length—it's not short like in Fenway Park. I mean, you have to hit it hard to get it out to that part of the park, and he hit it like a right-handed pull hitter."

August 7

The Angels dispute that they were throwing in the towel at the trading deadline when disposing of catcher Martin Maldonado and second baseman Ian Kinsler. But when Ohtani threw with a towel, that was a cause for celebration, not consternation.

It was a two-way day of positive results for the Angels' two-way star as he accelerated his rehabilitation from his elbow injury by executing his throwing motion with a towel in the bullpen before the game.

Then he went out and slugged his 12th home run on the year.

Ohtani, who last pitched on June 6, had previously extended his distance to 120 feet in his long-toss program while throwing on flat ground. The next box he needed to check off was "dry" throwing with a towel on the mound to get his body used to its slope.

If that goes well, the plan is for Ohtani to have a bullpen session on August 11. Not what Scioscia would describe as a "full gorilla" bullpen, but more of a "touch and feel" session.

"It will be the beginning stages of throwing off the mound, so the effort level will be monitored, and the reps will be monitored," Scioscia told mlb.com.

Predictably, Ohtani was ecstatic. He's aiming to pitch again in the season's final month, and, like he has done time and again, he may have his own September surprise.

"I've been waiting for this day," Ohtani told mlb.com. "I've been very eager, ever since I got injured. I'm very excited. Looking forward to it. Just hoping there's good results and no setbacks."

Little went wrong during the game for Ohtani, as well. He slugged a first-inning, three-run homer off Detroit Tigers righty Jacob Turner that helped turn the game into an early rout, with the Angels prevailing, 11–5.

Ohtani's 411-foot blast was impressive for its distance and its direction as he launched it over the left-field fence.

It was notable in that most of Ohtani's homers are to center or right-center. He reached a dozen round-trippers by giving a little love, and a home run ball, to his teammates in left field.

This Ohtani missile headed for the Angels bullpen, and the ease with which he sent a 91-mph fastball that far, that way, was difficult to ignore.

Ohtani is one smooth operator with a bat in his hands.

"It may look like I'm taking easy hacks, but I'm swinging the bat pretty hard," he said. "If it looks like [there is little effort] and the ball's flying far, that's a good sign. My timing is good. I'm seeing the ball well."

Scioscia said the position of Ohtani's bat when he makes contact causes the deception that he's barely getting the bat through the hitting zone.

"He leverages the ball very well," he said. "He's got great leverage in his swing. When he gets extended and barrels it up, the ball comes out very hot."

The Angels aren't creating much of a sizzle in the AL West, but Ohtani continues to punish pitchers from the AL Central. Of his 12 home runs, all but four have come against AL Central hurlers.

Ohtani has handled that division's pitchers, and he has a handle again on his dream of being a two-way star in the majors as his rehabilitation goes full steam ahead.

"People say I could maximize my potential by focusing on pitching or focusing on hitting but they don't know that," he told Kyodo News in early 2017. "There's no guarantee that I will be better at either."

August 11

To No. 17, the number 23 meant everything.

That was the amount of soft pitches Ohtani heaved in a bullpen session, his first since departing the Angel Stadium mound on June 6. That next day, Ohtani was diagnosed with a sprained elbow ligament, and his climbing atop a mound again in 2018 seemed doubtful.

Then again, this is Ohtani.

So there he was, hours before the game and even before the stadium gates were open, delivering various pitches in the Angels bullpen. Ohtani's offerings weren't popping the glove or making people's jaws drop, which can be the case with his assortment of pitches.

But even if it was a hyped version of just playing catch, it was significant.

"Today was a big first step," he told mlb.com. "Everything went well, so I'm just going to keep taking the next steps to get back."

The Angels remain hopeful, based on their staff's medical reports, that Ohtani can avoid Tommy John surgery after receiving platelet-rich plasma and stem-cell injections into his valuable right elbow. If he undergoes an operation or his elbow gives way, he wouldn't be able to pitch in 2019.

So far, the Angels plan to avoid that scenario is being kept alive. The anxious Ohtani continues to make strides at a pace prescribed by the team.

"He's been terrific," manager Mike Scioscia said. "I think that he's feeling very, very comfortable with the fact that everything is sound in his elbow. As we continue to test it moving forward in the next couple weeks, we'll get a better idea of exactly where he is."

Where did Ohtani go after his bullpen session? Rummaging around the bat rack to grab some wood as he prepared to be the Angels' designated hitter in their game against the Oakland A's.

But most were more interested in what Ohtani did when throwing a ball rather than trying to hit one. Still, Scioscia did his best to ease the excitement over his right-hander's potential return.

"It's something you can't force," Scioscia said. "It's not worth trying to get peace of mind and putting yourself at risk. All of these injuries will heal on their own time. I do think that it is important for a pitcher, coming out of this season, to know they're healthy. It gives them, I think, a leg up in the winter, and then going into spring training, they're ready to go."

Since Ohtani's arm injury, the Angels have said he could pitch again this season if cleared medically.

But others wondered if the team should risk his mending elbow in the season's final month with so little at stake.

It's clear Ohtani wants to throw again, but whether that is the prudent course of action is the question. There's no doubt how much he enjoys being on the mound.

"I saw a smile on his face, and I love that the ball was coming out of his hand quickly," Angels broadcaster Mark Gubicza said on Fox Sports West after an Ohtani bullpen session. "Whether that is the right thing or not remains to be seen."

What's not a cinch, if Ohtani doesn't test his tender elbow, is determining how the Angels would attack the offseason. With the rash of injuries to their starting pitchers, a late-season mound appearance by Ohtani could ease their worries about having to possibly replace him, too.

"It's the nature of the injury," said former Angels slugger Tim Salmon on Fox Sports West. "You really don't know what you have. I think the Angels need to know coming into this offseason whether or not he's going to available next year.

"You think about the moves they have to make in the offseason to put together a pitching staff, and you want to know going in that winter and those discussions whether this guy is healthy or not.

"This is an injury that might have a chance to blow. You'd rather have [his elbow] blow now rather than come back to spring training, have him dialed into your rotation, and then have an injury at the start of the season."

But José Mota, a colleague of Gubicza and Salmon, thinks the Angels should pump the brakes on Ohtani's return.

"Personally, I would love to see him not pitch this season," Mota said. "But if he is ready and he goes through every single one of those steps, then get him on the mound and see how he reacts from one outing to another. But in terms of where the Angels are in the standings and projecting forward, I would prefer he not take that chance."

August 14

The neighborhood around Petco Park has undergone a stunning transformation in the last 15 years. With the addition of the San Diego Padres' downtown ballpark, blocks have been upgraded from run-down to top-shelf.

Maybe it was a good spot for Shohei Ohtani as he strolled out to the visitors' bullpen on this summer afternoon.

Ohtani was looking to reinvent himself, too.

It was Ohtani's second bullpen session since the Angels put him on the shelf on June 7. He was to test his mending ligament in his precious right elbow again, and it was a quite a sight to see Japan's finest pitcher trying to get loose in America's Finest City.

It was clear this outing, while far from what manager Mike Scioscia calls a "full gorilla" event, was a step up in the Petco Park visitors' bullpen from the soft tosses Ohtani made recently at Angel Stadium.

Maybe it's a sign from heaven, at the home of the Friars, that Ohtani's pitching will be resurrected after a clean 33 pitches at about 70 percent. He stayed mostly with fastballs, although he did heave three curveballs and three sliders into the mix with interpreter Ippei Mizuhara videotaping Ohtani's effort.

What Ohtani didn't attempt was his wipeout splitter, and that could be taken two ways.

Ohtani suggests that pitch doesn't need as much work as his other offerings, which rely more on feel than power. But others wonder if he is avoiding the splitter because of the stress it puts on his arm.

"Everything went pretty well, just as I expected," Ohtani told mlb.com. "It was a step forward, and that is a good sign."

"I just wanted to get the feel of the mound," he said. "We will see how it feels tomorrow."

How did it feel today?

"This was a very big step for me, and I was able to clear it," Ohtani said. "I am moving forward, and hopefully I will be able to pitch again this season."

In San Diego, Ohtani ran into Padres reliever Kazuhisa Makita, another Japanese pitcher formerly with Nippon Professional Baseball. The two shared a conversation and a laugh before the game.

"It's been a while since I'd last seen him, and I just asked him what he had been up to lately," Ohtani said.

Makita had been busy, much like Ohtani. Although while Makita is constantly fighting for a roster spot, Ohtani is trying to accomplish feats last done by Babe Ruth, a century ago.

August 20

The progression of Shohei Ohtani's throwing program took a meaningful stride as minor-league hitters stepped into the batter's box for the first time to face him since he exited the Angel Stadium mound on June 6 with a sprained elbow ligament.

That the mound was at the team's Arizona spring training facility, and not the one at Chase Field, where the Angels were set to face the Diamondbacks the following day, wasn't that critical. Instead, the Angels were upbeat that Ohtani continues to move in the right direction in the hopes of pitching again before the season concludes next month.

August 21

Manager Mike Scioscia, as usual, cautioned those wanting to jump too far ahead in Shohei Ohtani's rehabilitation when meeting with the media for the first time since Ohtani threw a two-inning simulated game the previous day.

As Scioscia hopes Ohtani does, he urges others to take it slow.

Scioscia said his right-hander must first prove he can throw all of his pitches—fastball, splitter, sinker, and curveball—at 100 percent and at a certain workload properly test his elbow.

"Until that happens, there is no sense talking about when he will face hitters or let's think about when there will be a rehab start," he told Fox Sports West. "This process is going to take a while before we can evaluate exactly where he is."

Before the Angels kicked off a two-game series with Arizona, Ohtani spoke about his 29-pitch throwing session.

"I would love to go back out there [and pitch] any day, as soon as possible," Ohtani told the *Orange County Register*. "Of course, I know I can't do that. I have to take the right steps. Everything is going well so far. Hopefully, if it keeps up, it should hopefully be soon."

Ohtani will have another simulated game next week, according to Scioscia, with a 45-pitch limit.

I would love to go back out there [and pitch] any day, as soon as possible."

—Shohei Ohtani

August 22

After Shohei Ohtani's performance at Tempe Diablo Stadium, and his follow-up sessions, someone would have a devil of a time diffusing the optimism in manager Mike Scioscia's voice.

"Shohei had a great workout day today," he told mlb.com. "Energy level was great. He felt good coming out of it. His postworkout tests were encouraging. It was definitely a step in the right direction."

It's one small step for Ohanti and a giant leap in enthusiasm from his skipper. Scioscia is keen on minimizing expectations, but even he revealed how promising the future looks for Ohtani to pitch again this season.

Ohtani is bent on continuing his historic season as a hitter and a pitcher. He's been restricted from throwing in a game since June 6 and is slowly climbing his way back to a possible return before the season ends.

One season leads to another, according to Scioscia, and that's why it's important for Ohtani to prove his fitness level.

If, above all else, he's up to the task.

"You would never push him," Scioscia added. "You are not going to put a guy at risk, but there are definitely some big advantages to seeing where you are before the season ends.

"One of the black holes players have, and I've been hurt at the end of the year when I was playing, too, you never get a chance to set it. You never know where you are. You have to wait until spring training."

Angels fans can't wait that long, longing to see Ohtani back, shooting his lean and athletic 6-foot-4 frame toward home plate in leading the way for his disarming arsenal.

It looks like their wish will be granted as Ohtani continues to gain ground on what he must accomplish to return. If he is fit, the Angels won't ship him out for a minor-league rehabilitation assignment. That would require Ohtani going on the disabled list for 10 days, and the Angels don't want to be without his bat over that length of time.

"I don't believe we are going to wait for him to get stretched out to 100 pitches before he pitches in a major-league game," Scioscia said. "We're going to let this thing go organically. We're not going to look at a schedule and say he has to get here. It's going to be when he's ready."

Ready or not isn't the Angels' motto with Ohtani. But if he's ready, why not let him prove his arm is sound before some five months without competition?

"When a player pitches and he has peace of mind that he is healthy, it gives him much more direction in the offseason with what he needs to do," Scioscia said. "There are definitely some positives to find out where Shohei is."

August 24

After an offday, Shohei Ohtani was set to welcome an old friend with the world champion Houston Astros arriving for a three-game series. The catch is that Ohtani's pal is the catcher for the visitors, Martin Maldonado.

Ohtani's first batterymate was back in town after being traded to the Astros last month. When Ohtani and Maldonado laid eyes on each other behind the batting cage before the game, their bond was as clear as the playful jabs Maldonado delivered to Ohtani's muscular body.

"I used to do that every once in a while," Maldonado said with a grin.

Maldonado's task in spring training was a tall one. He had to learn how to catch Ohtani, a pitcher he had never seen before and one who came armed from Japan with four effective pitches.

It was estimated that Maldonado, who also had to overcome a language barrier with the new pitcher, studied more than 200 hours of Ohtani's outings in Japan.

"I had no idea about him," Maldonado said. "It was hard as a catcher to figure out stuff about him. He has a lot of pitches. I watched a lot of video of him, then there were a lot of bullpen sessions in the spring and I would catch his batting practices."

It was during the spring that Ohtani struggled, with many wondering if his two-way game would play in the majors.

Maldonado was among those hoping for the best once the season started, but like others, he wasn't sure what the results would be.

"At the same time, you knew he was getting people out in Japan and doing it well," Maldonado said. "That was something to look forward to. But there were question marks about him. But he turned out great."

At every turn some two hours before the first pitch, Ohtani and Maldonado were taking turns giving each other the business. In what language and how well each was speaking, it couldn't be heard.

"He knows some Spanish," Maldonado said. "He knows the basics and a couple of bad words, too."

How is Maldonado's Japanese?

"I knew just a couple of words," he said. "That's why he has his translator, and Ippei [Mizuhara] does a nice job. He was always there talking with us, and that made my job easier."

While others have a hard time grasping what Ohtani is trying to accomplish, he has a steady and consistent supporter in Maldonado.

"It was fun seeing him play both ways of the game," Maldonado said. "It was fun catching him, it was fun watching him hit. What people don't realize and what's amazing is how smart he is. That makes him even better."

The Astros got the better of the Angels, winning the opening game of the weekend series, 9–3. It was the first of a 1980s-themed weekend series, with the Angels players' faces being placed on movie trailers from that decade.

When Ohtani came to the plate, his mug was plastered over Tom Cruise's for *Top Gun*.

With it being Players' Weekend as well, they picked their nickname to grace the back of their jersey. Ohtani's read SHOWTIME.

But with the Angels trying to get back into the game with two on in the eighth inning, Ohtani chased a pitch to strike out and end the threat. Still, the show must go on, and there were plenty of fireworks between the teams in the following game.

August 25

On a warm Saturday night in Anaheim, there wasn't much love in the air between the Angels and Astros.

The Angels had to tangle with Houston right-hander Justin Verlander, and that's never done with ease. He had run his streak of scoreless innings at Angel Stadium to 26 before Ohtani dug his cleats into the disheveled dirt of the batter's box.

Verlander, known for his power pitches, tried to get cute by attempting to sneak a changeup past Ohtani. But Verlander's offering never found catcher Martin Maldonado's mitt as Ohtani kept his hands back and patiently waited for the pitch to come within striking distance.

When making contact with the baseball floating in at 87 mph after it pierced the center of the plate, Ohtani shot it out toward the left-center field fence and over it for a two-run blast.

"Big Fly, Ohtani-san!" Angels TV broadcaster Victor Rojas shouted into his microphone.

Ohtani's 14th home run of the season came one at-bat after he doubled off Verlander. Verlander had also tried to trick Ohtani during that duel, and instead it ended up turning into another Ohtani treat for Angels fans.

"I've been trying to work my changeup into my repertoire more," Verlander told mlb.com. "Threw it to [Ohtani], and obviously saw it very well, he saw it right out of my hand and was able to make an adjustment. He's got tremendous power."

But Ohtani's production came with a cost. The nightly fireworks Disneyland sets off each summer night had some company this evening.

Things got hot at Angel Stadium during Ohtani's final at-bat. Reliever Roberto Osuna peeked in for the sign and the target. But instead of hitting Maldonado's glove, Osuna plunked Ohtani in the middle of his lower back with a 97-mph bullet.

The umpires thought Ohtani was hit in retaliation for American League MVP José Altuve, the Astros' second baseman, getting nailed earlier in the game. Warnings were issued to both benches that there would be repercussions if another batter was struck.

But that didn't stop the Angels' Deck McGuire from hitting Yuli Gurriel in the leg in the ninth inning. McGuire was ejected, along with manager Mike Scioscia.

McGuire was sending a message as well as an errant fastball: don't mess with Ohtani, as we will protect our prized rookie if forced to do so.

"I would like to not think it was on purpose," Ohtani said. "I'm not sure about that. We hit their guy. I'm sure that wasn't on purpose. Hit by pitches are part of baseball. It happens. I'm not thinking about it too much."

His 14th long fly got some thinking about Ohtani's home run standard during his MVP season in the Nippon Professional Baseball in 2016. His rate of a home run in every 18 plate appearances is only slightly lower than his best season with the Ham Fighters.

August 26

The Angels lost their last meeting with the Astros, and Shohei Ohtani lost his rematch with Roberto Osuna.

Less than 24 hours from taking Osuna's fastball in the back, Osuna struck out Ohtani in his lone at-bat for the game's final out.

What was quirky on this day was Ohtani's face on *The Breakfast Club* movie trailer for the 1980s celebration the Angels were having. And when teammate David Fletcher came to bat, his walk-up song was "The Power of Love" by Huey Lewis and the News.

When Ohtani was an 18-year-old rookie in Japan, that was his first walk-up song. Now Ohtani was hearing it again in a different league, halfway across the world.

August 27

It seemed that the Angels had been flying in the wrong direction forever. The team had gone 51 consecutive innings without holding a lead when Shohei Ohtani stared out at Rockies pitcher Jon Gray in the fourth inning, after the Angels had gone without a hit in the first three frames.

Gray, his long blond hair looking to escape any opening in his hat, put a fastball within Ohtani's reach. He pounced on it for his 15th home run of the season, a 412-foot shot that gave the Angels a lead.

With his impressive blast, Ohtani became only the fourth player in major-league history to record 15 home runs and three pitching outings in a season.

What was also noteworthy was that his long fly came after throwing a lengthy simulated game consisting of 50 pitches.

"Personally, I feel like I don't need any more simulated games, but that's not up to me, ultimately," Ohtani told mlb.com. "It's going to be up to the coaching staff and the training staff, so I have to talk to them first."

All indications are that Ohtani's Grade 2 sprain of his ulnar collateral ligament in his right elbow is mending.

"I was always confident that I would be able to pitch sometime during the season," Ohtani said. "Every step, I'm getting closer and closer, so I'm feeling more confident."

Ohtani completed the three-ups session, which mimicked him going out for three innings with breaks in between.

"There are so may positives you can take away from it," manager Mike Scioscia said. "The velocity was really good. It's a step forward. We'll see how he's evaluated in the next couple of days and then what the next step is."

August 30

If the waiting really is the hardest part, it was at least finally over. Shohei Ohtani was given two thumbs up in returning to the mound in his bid to regain his status as a two-way player.

Manager Mike Scioscia announced that Ohtani would start against the Houston Astros on Sunday in his first pitching appearance since suffering a Grade 2 sprain of his right elbow's ulnar collateral ligament on June 6.

OHTANI ENTERS AUGUST LOOKING TO GET RIGHT AGAINST LEFTIES

Ohtani felt the Angels were being overly cautious in his return, as he noted he pitched with this injury in Japan. But the Angels didn't want to rush him back, and Ohtani, always a team player, didn't protest too much about being handled with care.

"I always wanted to get back on the mound as soon as I could," he told the *Orange County Register*. "Especially with all our starting pitchers getting hurt, going on the DL, it made me want to get back out there even more.

"Hopefully, I can finish the year strong, with a month left, with no setbacks or injuries."

Ohtani was sensational before his elbow revolted, compiling a 4–1 record with a 3.10 ERA and averaging 11.1 strikeouts in nine innings.

Scioscia, as usual, is preaching patience with Ohtani's results.

"I don't know if we can put those expectations to Shohei to when he started to hit stride, to have those expectations for what he's going to do on Sunday," Scioscia said, as Ohtani had fashioned a 2.17 ERA in his last five outings. "Hopefully, he's going to get back to that."

CHAPTER 14

A SEPTEMBER TO REMEMBER

September 2

Shohei Ohtani headed toward the mound to start a game for the first time since June 6, when he suffered a Grade 2 sprain of the ulnar collateral ligament in his right elbow.

But when beginning the stroll back to the dugout, with his warm-up pitches completed in the bullpen, Ohtani stopped dead in his tracks.

Something serious caused him to halt his graceful gait, and it was important for him to pause.

Yep, a discarded gum wrapper on the Minute Maid Field turf seized Ohtani's attention. He broke his stride to collect the wisp of trash and deposited it into his back pocket.

Ohtani's actions revealed a glimpse of what drives the two-way star and maybe why he is so popular. While others dissect and devour his every baseball move, it's clear there's more to the man than the game itself.

While nothing drives him more than wanting to excel, he never forgets his upbringing or his dedication to be the best person he can be. He's amiable and cares for others. So, in his mind, if he collected the gum wrapper, that meant someone else wouldn't have to be troubled by it.

It's no problem in Houston, or anywhere else, for him to give the extra effort off the field nearly as much as he does on it.

When Ohtani reached the mound in going to work against the Astros, the electricity in the stadium equaled a postseason contest. Not only was the venue packed and buzzing, but Ohtani's outing—another "Sunday with Shohei"—was being televised nationwide and, dare we say, worldwide with an audience in Japan, as well.

His postgame audience was also huge, with reporters from all over the globe eager for an update.

"I was more nervous than I thought I would be," said Ohtani, who had been restricted to hitting since June 6. "That goes for my degree of readiness, too. I was not at any kind of a high level."

The stakes were elevated as Ohtani toed the rubber for the first time in nearly 90 days. The right-hander was eager to prove the injections of platelet-rich plasma and stem-cell therapy on his right elbow would allow him to avoid Tommy John surgery.

"If I am at all able to throw, I want to pitch," he said. "My stance on that has never changed. If I was able to pitch this season, then that was something I had to do."

If he could clear the pitching hurdles in the campaign's final month, the Angels would be relatively confident he could be in their 2019 rotation.

If I am at all able to throw, I want to pitch."

—Shohei Ohtani

If his elbow balked, Ohtani would have to undergo the Tommy John operation, which would prevent him from pitching next season.

So Ohtani went to work against the Astros on a 50-pitch count, with the hope his prized arm could withstand the rigors of his fastball, which reaches triple figures, and the torque from his wipeout splitter.

After two scoreless innings, Ohtani was erasing the doubt that he could pull this off. His fastball was sitting around 96–97 mph.

"I didn't expect to throw that hard," he said. "But you know what? When all those people come to a game at this level, you just get amped up and that's that.

"Compared to practice, I was throwing a lot harder, putting my body into it, and that is a big thing."

Angels manager Mike Scioscia saw enough positive signs, and to him that overshadowed Ohtani taking the loss, to dropping his record to 4–2.

"The first two innings were electric," Scioscia said. "That's what you would expect."

Ohtani wiggled out of a first-inning jam when he froze Tyler White on a two-strike slider after earlier flashing a 99.3 mph fastball.

The second inning was pristine, as Ohtani retired the Astros in order, although the world champions did nick him when he attempted to field Marwin Gonzalez's comebacker with his pitching hand.

Scioscia, who's added some heft since his playing days, bolted from the dugout as if shot from a cannon to check on Ohtani.

"I haven't seen Mike move that fast since the 1988 World Series," joked Alex Rodriguez on the ESPN telecast.

Ohtani was almost too quick for his own good.

"I somehow felt I could catch it, so I stuck my hand out," Ohtani said. "Of course, it would have been better not to have done that, but it is important to strive to get every single out."

Then came the third inning, and the decrease in Ohtani's velocity was telling. His fastball was still spinning the radar gun, but at some 5 mph slower than in the opening two innings.

George Springer blasted a two-run homer off an elevated slider, and after 2 1/3 innings and 49 pitches, Ohtani's night was done.

Springer was battling Ohtani during the game, but after it, he was pulling for him.

"The velocity drop was probably obvious," Springer said. "He was at 98, 99, and when [the speed decrease] is that obvious, I hope he's OK."

Ohtani was replaced, and he made that slow trek back to the dugout in one of only a handful of games this season in which things didn't go the rookie's way.

"Third inning, obviously, his stuff wasn't as crisp," Scioscia said. "In talking to our medical staff, his back was a little tight. And when he took the ball off his ring finger, it just started to get a little bit sore. There was definitely a drop in velocity, but not connected at all to the thing that he had with his elbow before."

Ohtani fans exhaled but were also reminded of the early diagnosis when Ohtani exited his start against the Kansas City Royals on June 6. The Angels said the right-hander left that game because of a recurrence of blisters on his finger that had derailed his start versus the Boston Red Sox on April 17.

But after that Red Sox outing, Ohtani noted his right elbow was stiff, and an MRI revealed a Grade 2 sprain to an elbow ligament.

Ohtani was unsure on how he felt in his postgame remarks.

"I can't really say much at this point," he said. "I've got to see how my body reacts."

He also mentioned the grounder that ricocheted off his finger. That had Angels boosters crossing their fingers that might be the cause for the velocity drop on his fastball.

"When the ball made contact with my fingers, at first, I didn't really feel any pain or anything," he said. "I just kept on throwing. But as the inning went on and it got to the third inning, I started to feel [discomfort] in the finger area. Maybe that had something to do with the dip in velocity."

Ohtani tried to coax more from other pitches as his fastball betrayed him. But ultimately it wasn't enough.

"It was kind of hard getting through it with the low velocity, but I was trying to fight through it," he said. "I was trying to get out of that inning within that pitch count [50], but obviously I gave up that two-run homer, so I was disappointed."

Regardless, the start etched Ohtani's name in the record books yet again. He joined Babe Ruth as the only players in MLB history to pitch 50 innings and hit 15 homers in the same season.

BYPASSED BY OHTANI, TWO MANAGERS STILL OFFER PRAISE

Former Rangers manager Jeff Banister and ex-Giants skipper Bruce Bochy (who's now the Rangers manager), two baseball lifers, rolled through Petco Park late in the season with Shohei Ohtani still on their minds.

Both of their teams made spirited runs at signing Ohtani in the off-season, as they were among the seven finalists he chose from. But the Angels were his organization of choice, which possibly set in motion a series of events that ordained the Rangers and Giants to finish below .500 this season.

The finish line for the Rangers' disappointing season was finally in sight. A team that had won consecutive AL West titles in 2015 and '16 was playing out the string, concerned about building for the future.

Banister wondered what might have been if Ohtani had once again followed the path of his pitching idol, Yu Darvish. Darvish, like Ohtani, began his Nippon Professional Baseball career with the Ham Fighters and then started his life in Major League Baseball with the Rangers.

But Ohtani leaned toward the West Coast, which had Banister leaning back and rubbing his tanned face, which was marked by the lines of being in pro ball since 1986.

What still strikes Banister about Ohtani was his focus when he met with Rangers officials before selecting the Angels.

"First of all, he is a great athlete," said Banister, who would be dismissed as manager before the season ended. "But when I looked him right in the eye and talked directly to him, I was as impressed with him as with any young athlete I've ever been around."

The Rangers' due diligence on Ohtani was thorough. In every step of their investigation of the two-way star, it unearthed a one-way street of positive news.

"Our guys did extensive background on him, talking to his high school coach and the people around him," Banister said. "And this was a young guy that seemed to be extremely intelligent but was also willing to go the extra step to be in control. He was that disciplined.

"There was no doubt in our mind that this was a championship player when you add what he can do physically, along with the mental attitude."

Banister walked across the diamond and shook hands with Ohtani when the Rangers and Angels met in April. Since then, Banister has watched as Ohtani navigated a rookie season that produced statistics not seen in some 100 years. Some of those numbers have come at the Rangers' expense, with Ohtani going 19-for-57 against Texas, which includes six home runs and a four-hit game.

"To watch the transition from him coming from Japan to Major League Baseball and how he got comfortable throughout the year was something," Banister said. "Now this guy is a star player. He's fun to watch because he combines speed with power and, obviously, the ability to pitch."

That part of Ohtani's game was put on hold after an abbreviated start against the Houston Astros on September 2. A damaged elbow ligament forced the right-hander to have it surgically repaired on Monday, October 1, keeping him from the mound until 2020.

"Even with him having to go through the Tommy John stuff, this guy is going to come out on the back side of that and be as good as anybody," Banister said.

The Giants were great in 2010, 2012, and 2014 while winning the World Series. They were geared to make another run this year, eschewing the notion of tanking for the lure of obtaining prospects that may, or may not, lead to success.

San Francisco went with veterans this year in its hopes to recapture its glorious past, with Ohtani being a younger piece of the puzzle.

But Bochy knew the Giants were at a disadvantage as a National League club. Along with the Chicago Cubs and Los Angeles Dodgers, two other teams that made Ohtani's cut, they couldn't offer him the designated hitter role to complement his pitching.

"I know it would have been difficult for him to play two ways in the National League," Bochy said. "We would have had to get creative to make it work in how we used him. It's a little bit easier for him with the designated hitter in the American League because he hadn't been playing a lot of outfield his last year in Japan."

Bochy, like Banister as well as millions of baseball fans around the world, can't take their eyes off Ohtani. What really got Bochy's attention was his flexibility, and he's not talking about how limber the 6-foot-4 Ohtani is.

Bochy remembered when Ohtani was scuffling during spring training, with his high leg kick to start his swing compromising his ability to hit fastballs.

Instead of being stubborn and staying with what worked in NPB, Ohtani tinkered with his approach and chose to spin on his right foot instead of lifting it.

"It was a great adjustment he made with the hitting part," Bochy said. "Getting the foot down early, that really changed how he started hitting the ball.

"And of course, he has that gift on the mound. I know that he is dealing with something right now. But he is young, and he'll have time to overcome that."

Maybe if Ohtani had signed with the Rangers or Giants, they wouldn't be surrendering to a season that was filled with more losses than wins. But each manager said the Angels got a winner in Ohtani.

"I think he is a great athlete, and I think he made the right choice," Bochy said.

Another wise decision, according to Banister, would be if Ohtani pays close attention to teammate Mike Trout. Banister pointed to the joy Adrian Beltre, his third baseman with more than 3,000 hits, was playing with in his pregame drills.

Beltre's attention to detail was evident, as was a zest for the game that hasn't dimmed after 21 seasons.

"Ohtani has got a pretty good one with him in Trout," Banister said. "If you ever want to watch two guys, between Trout and Beltre, they have fun, they love playing the game.

"They keep that boyhood charm to them, and they have a great time playing. Those two players are a great example of how Ohtani should approach it."

September 4

The day after Shohei Ohtani's return to the mound came with arm concerns, but the right-hander didn't seem fazed.

"It's a little sore because I threw yesterday in a live game situation, but it's nothing out of the norm," Ohtani told the *Orange County Register*. "I'll see from here and try to prepare for the next start."

That would be the following Sunday in Chicago against the White Sox.

But there were some flashing warning lights with Ohtani. His fastballs in the first two innings were reaching the plate at 95–99 mph, but in the third, they dropped to 91–92. He had a similar decrease in speed in his outing on June 6, when he first hurt his elbow this season.

"Naturally, a red flag goes up, especially with what happened last time," Scioscia said. "But Shohei said he felt great. He had no apprehension about what was happening in his elbow."

September 4

Shohei Ohtani was back in the batter's box after taking a game off, following his custom of not hitting on days after he pitches. He was facing a southpaw starter in Texas's Mike Minor, and lefties were a challenge for Ohtani.

After going down on strikes in his first two at-bats, Ohtani came to the plate leading off the sixth inning with the Angels facing a 4–1 deficit.

Minor tried to tempt Ohtani with a sweeping slider, but it consumed too much of the plate. Ohtani attacked the offering and sent it into the right-center-field seats for his 16th home run of the year, but more important, his first long fly off a lefty this season.

With the blast, Ohtani also tied his hitting idol, Hideki Matsui, for the second-most homers by a Japanese player in his rookie year in the majors, with Matsui doing it with the New York Yankees in 2003. Now Ohtani set his sights on Kenji Johjima's mark of 18, which was established in 2006 when he played for the Seattle Mariners.

September 5

The statement on Angels letterhead arrived, with each sentence feeling like a punch in the gut. The Angels, and Shohei Ohtani's, worst fears had arrived with an MRI delivering a dour dose of news regarding the star right-hander's mending right elbow.

Angels doctors were recommending Ohtani consider Tommy John surgery to reconstruct his damaged ulnar collateral ligament.

Suddenly, Ohtani's dreams of being a two-way superstar were dashed, for a season anyway. The recovery period would erase his chances of pitching in 2019.

But the odds of Ohtani throwing a pity party for himself? Zilch. If Ohtani couldn't pitch, so be it. But he was cleared to bat, and he was determined to do that to the best of his ability.

His name was scribbled in the lineup, No. 17 holding down the No. 3 hole that night.

"He's a tough kid, not only physically, but mentally," Scioscia told mlb.com. "He understands the game, he understands the challenges. He knows he's talented, and tonight, he was a hitter."

Ohtani willingly ignored the devastating developments regarding his pitching and produced his second career four-hit game. This one included two home runs, adding to Ohtani's legacy.

Mark Langston called the game for the team's radio station AM 830 KLAA. The former major-league pitcher thought Ohtani was trying to lift the spirits of others, as well as his own, with his epic night at the plate.

"It was like he didn't want the negative news because it made everyone else sad," Langston said. "So he wanted to have some positive news, and he made that happen that night with his hitting. For him to do that so soon after hearing the news about his elbow, well, that was incredible."

It was also Ohtani being Ohtani, not wanting to be a burden to others. Instead, he went to work, even if his workload would unfortunately and temporarily be sliced in half.

"We still see him as a two-way player," general manager Billy Eppler said in a conference call.

While Ohtani's fans cursed his fate, Ohtani caught Johjima with his 18th homer. That's tied for the most by a Japanese player in his rookie season in the majors.

But his big night couldn't eclipse the afternoon's developments.

Ohtani had pitched for the final time in 2018, but he can hit, and that would absorb his steely focus.

"People will never understand how seriously he takes his job," shortstop Andrelton Simmons told mlb.com. "He comes in, he works. He does his homework, and he balls. He goes out there and impresses his teammates every day, really. It's nice to see he is still in good spirits. And he can hit a ball really, really hard."

September 7

Shohei Ohtani pushed his worries and his countryman Kenji Johjima aside as he continued his hot hitting against the Chicago White Sox.

Ohtani powered a three-run homer to help lead the Angels to a 5–2 victory. It was his fourth long fly in the last three games, all coming after he hurt his elbow pitching against the Houston Astros.

His latest homer, No. 19, set the mark for Japanese rookies, surpassing Johjima's standard set in 2006 as a Seattle Mariner.

People will never understand how seriously he takes his job."
—Shortstop Andrelton Simmons

"It's pretty cool that a two-way player, when you get injured doing one thing, you can do another," Mike Trout told mlb.com. "And it's pretty amazing how he could easily shut the season down, but he wants to finish out strong, and he works hard in the cage, and he works hard in general coming to the field. You know it's fun to watch, pretty incredible what he's doing right now."

Ohtani, of course, shrugged. He sees it as his duty as the ultimate team player to contribute in any way possible, despite having an injury that could easily have him opting out.

"He's got some big decisions coming up when we get back to Southern California," Scioscia said. "But he wants to play baseball. He goes out there, and he's excited to be in there and be able to swing the bat. He's playing very well."

Now he has to decide how to get well. All signs point to him undergoing Tommy John surgery, but Ohtani had yet to reach that verdict.

"Nothing is set right now," he told the *Orange County Register*. "I have a few options out there. I am still trying to look at every single option. I will make a decision sometime toward the end of the season."

Ohtani conceded that he navigated his historic rookie season's second half with doubt regarding his right arm's durability.

"Somewhere in the back of my mind, I was preparing to get Tommy John," he said. "That's something that was in the back of my mind the whole time."

But that didn't outweigh how blessed he was to still be batting. Angels doctors said with Ohtani being a left-handed pitcher and a right-handed batter, he'll be able to hit next season.

New York Yankees infielder Gleyber Torres, one of Ohtani's rivals in the American League Rookie of the Year race, bats and throws from the same sides as Ohtani. Torres was back hitting four months after his Tommy John surgery, a timetable that should have Ohtani ready around spring training.

"I'm trying to take it as positive as possible," Ohtani said, which is no surprise. "I'll still be able to hit next year, so I'll try to stay positive."

Remember the negative noise about Ohtani being unable to hit southpaws? Of those four homers in his past three games, two have come against lefties.

"Lately, when he's getting a pitch to hit from a lefty, he's hitting it hard," Scioscia told the *Orange County Register*. "The results are there. As we talked about it, it's just going to be a matter of him getting comfortable and seeing more lefties. He'll be fine. He's swinging it well against righties and lefties and everyone in the last week."

Deciphering southpaws wasn't an issue for Ohtani in Japan, and he doesn't expect it to be problem in the majors.

"The more at-bats I get, the more comfortable I feel, the better I see the ball," he said. "It's just seeing a lot of pitches over and over."

September 10

It was the second American League Player of the Week award for the Angels' two-way star, but it was his first while being exclusively a hitter.

So it goes for Shohei Ohtani as he claims an honor in a fashion that has never been done. After being selected for his pitching and hitting during April, it was his big bat that had Major League Baseball reaching out to the Angels with the announcement.

Ohtani had been raking at the plate in the week of games that ended the previous day. It was a tear of epic proportions as he batted .474 with four home runs and 10 RBIs.

That his outburst came after learning his elbow had been damaged to a degree that surgery was likely required made his work more impressive.

Instead of moping, Ohtani morphed into the American League's best hitter.

"I'm very humbled and honored by it," Ohtani said on the MLB Network. "Especially when I missed about six weeks with [an arm] injury, and I'm proud I was able to come back and be able to win this award again."

Again and again, Ohtani spreads his good vibes through baseball. Many viewers were likely seeing Ohtani being interviewed for the first time, and with the help of his interpreter, Ippei Mizuhara, his impeccable manners and thoughtfulness for others were on display.

When asked about the media demands he faces by having to accommodate dozens of Japanese reporters, he waved off the obstacle.

"I'm more worried about my teammates with there being so much Japanese media in the clubhouse, I am just hoping they are not bothered by it," he said.

That mind-set was similar to Ohtani's thinking when it was revealed his elbow had been damaged again. He saw the long faces in his clubhouse and went about turning those frowns around with a week of stellar baseball.

"I wasn't the only one that was kind of down, everyone that's around me, had supported me, they were down," he said. "So I want to send some good news and keep everyone in good spirits by performing well on the field, and I think I accomplished that."

Maybe it was Ohtani paying a tab from spring training, when others came to his aid. Few predicted Ohtani would be celebrating his second AL Player of the Week award when he couldn't retire minor-league hitters or master major-league pitching very well.

That seems like a long time ago. But what those in the Angels organization did for Ohtani in Arizona wasn't forgotten.

"I felt like the level of competition was much higher over here, and I felt that daily in every at-bat I took," Ohtani said, recalling those dark days in the Valley of the Sun.

"Maybe I was starting to lose a little confidence each day.

"But then Billy Eppler, the general manager, gave me a pep talk, and he said to stay confident and that you have all the abilities in the world and just believe in yourself. That helped me.

"Also the coaching staff and everyone on the team kept on giving me kind words and words of encouragement."

Even someone whom many considered among the game's most talented players needs an occasional pat on the backside.

"That helped me get through everything," Ohtani said.

Next, Ohtani had to get through nine innings. The Texas Rangers were in town, and it was time for Ohtani to go to work.

Showing few signs of slowing down from his wonderful week—on the field—he contributed two hits, an RBI, and a stolen base. The Angels, though, saw their four-game winning streak snapped, 5–2.

MAKITA PREDICTS OHTANI WILL ONLY GET BETTER

Padres pitcher Kazuhisa Makita shared a special day with Shohei Ohtani. Makita was playing for the Saitama Seibu Lions when Ohtani made his Nippon Professional Baseball debut with the Ham Fighters in 2013.

Although Makita doesn't remember there being much fuss about it.

"I don't recall any," he said through his interpreter, with a grin.

But Makita is certain about something else.

"I faced Shohei seven times in Japan, and he has never gotten a hit off me," he said.

Makita isn't surprised Ohtani was a smash in his first season with the Angels. The right-handed reliever said Ohtani's hitting and pitching skills were evident in Japan, as they are in the majors.

"Watching him play in Japan and then over here, with the success he has had it feels like he is a player that comes along once in a thousand years," said Makita, a two-time All-Star with the Lions. "He is one of those special players."

The Angels' star's unique approach to the game transcends the field. Makita was asked if the tales of Ohtani's unrelenting focus were true.

"Definitely," he said. "I even tried to ask him to go out and eat a couple of times in Japan. But he wouldn't go, he would make excuses or say he doesn't feel right. But again, it is just because he loves baseball so much that he is always working on his skills, where some guys would be more interested in dating women. But Shohei is the type of kid that everything is about baseball."

"Often players will have hobbies and do things they like that are outside of baseball. But for him everything is baseball. It is all he does. Outside of baseball, all he does is baseball. He is practicing, working on his game, and in its purest form, he just loves being around baseball constantly."

Even after Ohtani's reputation got punched around during a rocky spring training. Makita scoffed at those doubting Ohtani's prowess.

"Definitely he struggled, and there was a lot of negative press out there," Makita said. "But even a genius like Shohei struggles at times. It was just him getting acclimated, getting used to things, just trial and error. Once he figured it out, he was going to have success. It was just a matter of time."

As proof, Makita pointed to Ohtani ditching his high right leg kick while starting his hitting motion.

"The fastball velocity is much faster here," Makita said. "So Shohei made an adjustment."

Next year, Ohtani will be restricted to hitting, as his elbow injury prevents him from pitching. Like others, Makita would like to see Ohtani on the field as well as in the batter's box.

"It's hard to say if he is a better pitcher or hitter because he is special in both areas," he said. "But he has the elbow thing now, and if he would just focus on one, just hitting, he could probably go after some of the records in the major leagues."

But then he wouldn't be Ohtani, the two-way star with the bright future that does baseball on his terms.

"You really get good in baseball in your late twenties, and he is just 24," Makita said. "The sky is the limit with him. He is going to improve, and he is just going to get better and better. He is dedicated to his craft and the perfection part of it, where he is finding ways to improve upon improvement.

"There have been Japanese legends playing baseball, like Sadaharu Oh, Shigeo Nagashima, Ichiro [Suzuki], and [Hideo] Nomo. Shohei is right up there with those guys."

September 15

Troutani lives!

For the first time, Mike Trout and Shohei Ohtani collected back-to-back homers, but it wasn't enough to prevent the Angels from falling to the Seattle Mariners, 6–5.

Trout struck first, and five pitches later, as the revved Angels fans were settling back into their seats, Ohtani delivered a long fly.

A beaming Trout—looking more like a prideful big brother than a teammate—was waiting for Ohtani by the on-deck circle. He smartly removed Ohtani's helmet and then faked as if he were throwing it in the seats. Instead, he returned it to the dugout, where high fives and hugs had consumed No. 17.

For Ohtani, it was his 20th home run on the year, and, as is usually the case with the Japanese star, it was noteworthy.

Ohtani, who also had a single, joined Trout in being among eight Angels to notch 20 home runs in their rookie season. In an even bigger picture, Ohtani now had 10 pitching appearances with 20 blasts, and the last player to do that was George Herman "Babe" Ruth in 1919.

September 24

With Shohei Ohtani's lean, athletic frame, it's often easy to misread the strength of the designated hitter. There's some brawn underneath that Angels jersey, and Ohtani proved it on a Monday in Orange County.

Although Newport Beach was some 23 miles south from Angel Stadium, Ohtani turned Anaheim into Muscle Beach when squaring up his 21st homer in the Angels' 5–4 extra-inning victory over the Texas Rangers.

"I got all of the barrel," Ohtani told mlb.com. "I felt pretty good on how far it went."

Ohtani's 428-foot shot helped eased the pain of a recent 3-for-22 skid. Just like there was little doubt Ohtani would emerge from his slump, there was no question when Adrian Sampson's elevated sinker exited Ohtani's bat at 112.9 mph that it was a goner. It was the hardest-hit homer of Ohtani's major-league career.

September 26

Before Shohei Ohtani reported to work, he revealed his thoughts about the team's recommendation on September 5 that he undergo Tommy John surgery to repair his ulnar collateral ligament in his right elbow.

Ohtani agreed to have the operation the week after the season ends, and it was in fact performed by noted surgeon Dr. Neal ElAttrache.

Although Ohtani will be unable to pitch again until 2020, the plan has him resuming his duties at designated hitter.

"He'll be able to hit, and I think he is at peace with that," manager Mike Scioscia told the Associated Press. "He wants to excel at both phases of the game. The fact he can't pitch [in 2019], there is a little bit of a void. But he'll be able to hit and focus on that."

When the evening's game reached its later stages, a familiar face stared in at Ohtani. It was one that the Angels' star got to know when Texas Rangers reliever Chris Martin was in foreign land, instead of Ohtani.

Martin was Ohtani's teammate with the Fighters in Nippon Professional Baseball. For two seasons, they wore the same uniform, including the 2016 campaign, when the Nippon-Ham Fighters won the Japan Series over the Hiroshima Toyo Carp.

So, with the game on the line in the eighth inning, Martin was going to tiptoe around Ohtani. He knew firsthand of his hitting skills, and he was determined not to let Ohtani beat him.

Ohtani, who earlier had an RBI single against lefty Yohander Mendez, had only seen Martin try to get the best of other hitters. As his teammate, Ohtani had never faced Martin until climbing into the batter's box in a 2–2 game. As usual, the crowd stirred when Ohtani approached the plate after intently studying Martin in the moments leading to his at-bat.

"It was my first time facing him," Ohtani told mlb.com. "But I was able to see him from the on-deck circle and also earlier in the season. He had made really good pitches, but I was able to adjust pretty well during the at-bat."

Martin reared back, and the right-hander attempted to run a fastball over the outer part of the plate and past Ohtani. What came next wasn't so much a towering home run as a laser of a line drive that was either going to go over the left-field fence or pierce it.

"He left a pitch up in the zone, the last pitch, and I was able to swing through it," Ohtani said.

The big fly from Ohtani-san also was his 22nd on the year, matching his career high when he and Martin were sharing a Ham Fighters clubhouse in 2016.

That was Ohtani's best year as a hitter in the NPB. To equal that in his debut season in the majors has many believing he will be named the American League Rookie of the Year.

"I see it as two completely different things," Ohtani said. "Different countries, different ballparks, different balls. But being able to accomplish my career high in my first year in the big leagues is a huge thing for me. I'm proud of that."

Ohtani was embarrassed earlier in the year when Martin picked him off first as a pinch-runner. But this time, Ohtani got the upper hand, but Martin's hard feelings couldn't last too long. If not for Ohtani, it's possible Martin isn't in the majors.

Martin said he benefitted from being on Ohtani's team in Japan.

When scouts sat in the stands evaluating and salivating over the wonders of Ohtani, they also got a look at Martin.

"It helped me a lot," Martin told Fox Sports West. "There were a lot of guys over there watching Shohei play. I felt like if I pitched well, there was going to be a lot of major-league teams watching him and maybe get a peek at me and say, 'Hey, he is doing well, let's keep an eye on him while we are over here.' It worked out for the both of us."

Martin understands the challenges Ohtani faces being a stranger in a strange land. Although Ohtani seems to handle it as well as he did Martin's pitch that he sent into the bullpen.

"I don't think he really gets bothered by much," Martin said. "He is pretty focused on playing baseball, and that's pretty much what you got to do when in a foreign country. I've been in the same situation. You just focus on baseball."

When Ohtani's detractors highlighted his dreadful spring training numbers, Martin wasn't fazed. He had seen Ohtani win games almost single-handedly. In one, Martin said Ohtani led off the game with a homer and then threw eight scoreless innings.

"He's been playing since he was 18 at a professional level, so he knew what spring training was about," Martin said. "It's a learning curve, adapting to guys and how guys were going to pitch him and how they were going to approach him when he was pitching.

"He had to feel it out a little bit. When the season started, you switch on another gear, and he was no different."

What's odd is being a two-way star, and that's not lost on Martin.

"He is something that you don't see very often," Martin said. "I think you do see it over here, guys can do both. But ultimately, they make you chose one side or the other, so you become better at one or the other.

"In Japan they wanted him on the team and they said, 'We will let you hit and pitch,' like the Angels did, 'because you are a big asset on both sides.'"

But on this night, Ohtani was on the winning side. Only because Ohtani did everything but make Martin feel right at home.

September 28

The Angels were determined to end on a high note in the season's final weekend. When they beat the Oakland Athletics, 8–5, their winning streak reached four games, and Shohei Ohtani was right in the middle of the victory.

Ohtani went 3-for-3 and had two RBIs and a stolen base to pace the Angels, with Mike Trout adding his 39th homer on the year.

Those fishing for excuses why Ohtani doesn't deserve to be the AL Rookie of the Year need to listen to manager Mike Scioscia.

"In my mind, he's hands down Rookie of the Year," he told mlb.com. "I don't know if anyone's come into the league in a long time and done as much as he's done. Even though his pitching season was cut short, when he was out there, he was dominant. I think at the plate, you see the talent. He's having a terrific season."

Ohtani joined Devon White (1987) and Trout (2012) as the only Angels to hit 20 home runs and steal 10 bases in their first year.

Ohtani wasn't tapping the brakes, although the end was near.

"The way I finish the season is really important to me, whether it's good or bad," Ohtani said. "Because I know what to work on during the offseason."

September 30

The skipper was setting sail into another chapter of his life. Shohei Ohtani was determined he would go out on a positive vibe.

Mike Scioscia was managing his last game as he capped his 19th season at the helm for the Angels. But in his final outing, it appeared he was heading off into the Southern California sunset with a loss.

The Angels were trailing the visiting Oakland Athletics, 4–2, with the home nine down to their final three outs.

Ohtani's inning-opening single sparked a three-run rally, as he came around to score on Jefry Marté's double. Taylor Ward followed with a two-run homer, and suddenly what looked like a downer of a day with the curtain falling on the season flipped to walk-off triumph for Scioscia, the 1,650th of his career, which is 18th on the all-time managerial list.

OHTANI IS A GAME CHANGER WITH HIS TWO-WAY APPROACH

Tampa Bay Rays manager Kevin Cash said Shohei Ohtani could change the manner in which major-league organizations develop young players. He's all in on two-way players, and the Rays proved it in the 2017 MLB draft.

"I better be in that camp because we drafted a two-way player," Cash said. "I'm very much on board with it, and I think we will probably see more players like Shohei."

The Rays selected Brendan McKay fourth overall, a first baseman and left-handed pitcher out of the University of Louisville. Tampa Bay isn't eager to push him into one area or the other, instead letting him play both ways in the minors.

"In the past few years there has been plenty of guys at the college level that have done it, but they probably haven't been afforded the opportunity to do it at the professional level," Cash said. "I think we will see that trend start to change."

McKay eventually made it to the majors in 2019 and took a perfect game into the seventh inning in his debut. He would see playing time as a pitcher and a hitter, although not in the same games.

Unfortunately, various injuries stalled his development and he's currently in the Rays' minor-league system while rebounding from Tommy John surgery.

Spencer Jones, a lanky, athletic 6-foot-7, 210-pound teenager in Southern California, could be among the benefactors of how Ohtani has challenged the game's status quo. Jones was selected the MLB/ SiriusXM Two-Way High School Player of the Year, as he was a standout left-handed hitter and southpaw pitcher for La Costa Canyon High School in north San Diego County.

Jones, a senior and one of the nation's top prep players, earned a baseball scholarship to Vanderbilt University. But he's projected to go high in the draft, and so far, many of the scouts evaluating him encourage him to continue hitting and pitching.

"When we meet with teams regarding Spencer, they mention how the game is changing, and that they see him as a legitimate two-way player," said Chris Jones, Spencer's father. "I'm sensing a trend to it becoming more acceptable."

Thanks to Ohtani, maybe someday two-way players soon won't be so unique in the majors.

"I think it is awesome what he is doing and one of the coolest things to come out of baseball in a long time," Spencer Jones said. "It completely changes the way some people think of what a player can do, pitching and hitting, and it opens the door for two-way players.

"A couple of teams that I've talked to, they mention Ohtani and the success he has had. They think it's the future of baseball and maybe with the next generation of players it won't be that big of a deal. Whether it's a guy starting a game or coming in late in games to pitch an inning or two."

Jones continued that Ohtani reintroducing the concept of a two-way player after nearly a century without one is admirable.

"It's definitely hard being the first guy," he said. "I'm not surprised he is doing well; what surprises me is it took so long for someone to try it."

The Rays are among those willing to explore fresh ideas to win games.

"It will take really talented players to do it, but we will see teams going forward and pushing the envelope to see what they have," Cash said. "I think the value of having a player like Shohei has only grown since he has come over here and shown how good he is.

"I just think when you are looking at the value of it, you are getting one player that can fill multiple roles. So in theory, you've got a more versatile roster."

While Jones gave going both ways a shot, arm injuries put a road-block on his pitching career. Jones became exclusively a hitter at Vanderbilt and was the New York Yankees first-round pick of the 2022 draft.

The multiskilled Jones, 22, had hoped he could follow in Ohtani's trailblazing path.

"Honestly, I would love to do both beyond college because I don't think there are many guys that can do that," he said. "And being considered to be one of those guys is pretty special."

Ohtani Caps a Season Like No Other

Shohei Ohtani's remarkable season had come to a close, and it did so with some regret. Not from what might have been, although Ohtani's pitching was cut short because of an elbow injury, but because he delivered so much joy on a steady basis to baseball fans around the world.

It was a remarkable year, with him hitting .285 with 22 home runs, 61 RBIs, and a .925 on-base-plus slugging in 367 plate appearances. He added 10 stolen bases.

In 10 starts, he went 4–2 with a 3.31 ERA spread over 51 2/3 innings. He averaged 11 strikeouts per nine innings, finishing with 63 strikeouts in total.

It was the type of performance that shocked many, although manager Mike Scioscia wasn't among those rubbing his eyes.

"I wouldn't say he has exceeded anything," Scioscia told ESPN. "He's capable of doing everything we've seen him do on the field."

Ohtani, although he missed 22 games with an elbow injury, presents a compelling argument to win the Rookie of the Year Award. Along with Babe Ruth in 1919, only two players have had 10 pitching appearances and hit 20 home runs in the same season.

And only Ohtani did it as a rookie.

Just like there is only one world champion, and again this year it won't be the Angels. Despite the team's failure to reach the postseason, Ohtani said joining the Angels was the right call.

"I feel that I made the right decision, and I feel that I made that more every day that I come to the field," he told the *Orange County Register*. "Every game that I play, I feel more and more that I made the right decision."

Ohtani's smile seldom escaped his youthful face during the season. That includes the time after he learned his injured elbow would require Tommy John surgery.

"Overall, I was able to have fun and enjoy everything when I was playing on the field," he said. "That's a really good thing to take out of this season. Unfortunately, I'm very disappointed the team wasn't able to make the playoffs. I'll try to come back stronger next year, and hopefully next year we'll be in the playoffs."

Where Ohtani won't be in 2019 is on the mound after becoming the first player to strike out 50 batters and slug at least 20 homers in a season.

He'll be getting his surgically repaired elbow into shape next season, but at least he'll be able to hit.

But there is only one first year in the majors, and Ohtani, after finally reaching his lifetime goal, embraced it for all it was worth.

"I've learned so much, experienced so much, that it's hard to pick one thing," said Ohtani, who won the AL Rookie of the Month awards in April and September. "But one thing I can say for sure is that I gained a lot of experience as a baseball player, and I felt like I matured and grew."

❝

I'll try to come back stronger next year, and hopefully next year we'll be in the playoffs."

—Shohei Ohtani

The Angels' trophy case could be expanding as Ohtani bids to become the franchise's third Rookie of the Year, along with Tim Salmon (1993) and Mike Trout (2012).

"I try not to worry about the whole Rookie of the Year race," the typically modest Ohtani said. "We'll see what happens."

There's one more question begging for an answer: when, if ever, will there be another rookie season like Shohei Ohtani's?

CHAPTER 15

SHOHEI SHOWS OFF WITH AN UNPRECEDENTED MVP SEASON

There was a clue in spring 2021 that Shohei Ohtani was poised to do something extraordinary that year. The Angels were tuning up in Arizona, with Ohtani's engine already engaged at a high level. His Cactus League double-dip of greatness wasn't prickly, instead an appetizer of what was on the horizon.

Ohtani, nearly two and a half years removed from Tommy John surgery and now fully healthy, was facing Jose Abreu, the then-Chicago White Sox first baseman and the American League's Most Valuable Player in 2020. In a matchup between two of the game's brightest stars, Ohtani fanned Abreu.

About 72 hours later, Ohtani was digging in against Cleveland Indians right-hander Shane Bieber. Like Abreu, Bieber was honored after the previous season with the Cy Young Award as the AL's top pitcher.

Ohtani climbed into the box and rested his bat on his left shoulder, respectful of Bieber's hardware but hardwired to get the upper hand. Ohtani unleashed his powerful swing on a Bieber offering, and it was bye-bye baseball as it soared over the fence.

In striking out Abreu and homering off Bieber, two of the top players in the American League, Ohtani was teasing his fans that his best was yet to come.

Ohtani, of course, had revealed his immeasurable skills during his celebrated 2018 campaign when he was tabbed as the AL Rookie of the Year after playing five seasons in Japan.

He had proven himself through his eye-opening, two-way performances and revealed that those constant comparisons between him and the legendary Babe Ruth were more than baseball hyperbole.

But after Ohtani stunned the baseball world once again in 2021, with his varied excellence over the course of a demanding season, the Ruth-Ohtani narrative flipped.

Soon, Ruth was being held up to Ohtani's standards instead of the reverse.

Ohtani's MLB career reached overdrive in 2021 as he did this and that and darn near everything else. He played while sporting a constant smile as he exhibited a sense of endless joy that attracted millions of new Ohtani boosters around the world.

The fresh face of baseball was one exhibiting smooth skills, movie-star looks, and a child-like exuberance seldom seen at the game's highest level.

"I want to leave a strong impression as a player," Ohtani told *Time* magazine. "People say different things about me because I'm doing something unique. But I want to be a player that people remember."

When Ohtani tied a bow on his unforgettable season, he had slugged 46 homers, driven in 100 runs, compiled a .965 OPS, stole 26 bases, and had eight triples to tie for the AL lead.

Those numbers standing alone would have someone on the MVP podium, at least as a top-three finisher in the balloting.

But when Ohtani's impact from the mound is included, it's clear that his season was one of a kind—unless, Ohtani does it again.

As the Angels ace, Ohtani went 9–2 with a 3.18 ERA. Over his 23 starts, he worked 130 $\frac{1}{3}$ innings and recorded 156 strikeouts, which averages to nearly 11 over nine innings. His 46 earned runs allowed mirrored the 46 home runs he hit.

The Angels relish going into battle with Shohei, and a peek at his WAR rating—wins above replacement —tell the story why.

His 4.9 WAR mark as a hitter was the best in the majors. His 4.1 showing as a pitcher was also among baseball's elite.

Add them up and his 9.0 WAR eclipsed everyone else in MLB.

Thing is, Ohtani isn't like anyone else and that, in his eyes, skews what he accomplished in 2021.

"More than anything, I have no one to compare myself with," Ohtani said. "I could have a better understanding on how good my numbers are if there were more people like me and the sample size was bigger . . . so it's hard for me to understand where I stand."

While perched on Ruth's shoulders, if you will, Ohtani separated himself from his colleagues with a season that was as complete as it was crazy.

"Anything that Shohei does doesn't surprise me anymore," Trout told a reporter at that year's All-Star Game. "It's always something, every night."

Ohtani's unprecedented season arrived because the restrictions went away.

His was a delicate dance in his first three seasons with the Angels, as Ohtani and the organization were forging a path that hadn't been walked in a significant manner in nearly a century. Early in Ohtani's career with the Angels, he didn't hit on days he pitched, as well as the days before or after he took the mound.

But former Angels manager Joe Maddon, with Ohtani's blessing, tossed aside caution like Ohtani discarding his bat to retrieve his glove. Ohtani not only pitched and batted on the same, and consecutive days, but he played some outfield, too, after they sent in relief in order to keep his offensive prowess in the lineup.

Ohtani was certainly a presence at the All-Star Game with a mile-high list of accomplishments for being the first player to do numerous things. While some of baseball's grandest performers beg off from participating in the All-Star events, Ohtani went all in.

He competed in the Home Run Derby, he was the AL's starting pitcher, and he batted leadoff.

Outside the chalk lines, Ohtani did something even more incredible. He gifted the $150,000 he received from the Home Run Derby to the Angels' public relations staff and training team to divvy up among them.

Ohtani was money all season, so much so that designating a highlight or two from his work is a chore.

His bookends on the season is a good place to start, as he gave a tease in the opener against the Oakland Athletics.

In the first inning of the first game, Ohtani threw a pitch 100 mph. Also in the first inning, he belted a homer that exited the bat at 112 mph before coming to a rest some 450 feet away. No one had ever thrown a pitch and hit a ball that eclipsed 100 mph in a game, let alone in one inning.

The final game of his fantastic 2021 season, against the Seattle Mariners, was equally enticing. Batting first, Ohtani smoked a pitch 418 feet for his 46th homer and 100th RBI.

That would have him reaching, and in some instances exceeding, some incredible milestones on the year: 45 homers, 100 RBIs, 100 runs scored, 20 stolen bases, 100 innings pitched, and 150 strikeouts.

"There's just one person who could replicate that in the future and it is him," Maddon told reporters.

When the AL MVP votes were cast, one thing that rang true on all 30 ballots was Ohtani being named as the first-place finisher. It was but the 19th time in MVP history that a player had won in a unanimous fashion as Ohtani joined Don Baylor (1979), Vlad Guerrero (2004), and Trout (2014, '16, '19) to claim the coveted award with the Angels.

"Shohei's season was nothing short of electric," Trout said in a video message to the media. "At times, I felt like I was back in Little League. To watch a player throw eight innings, hit a home run, steal a base, and then go to right field was incredible. What impresses me the most with him, though, is the way he carries himself both on and off the field."

Ohtani's dream season for the ages changed the way others viewed him. Once the skeptics scoffed at Ohtani trying, let alone shining, in playing both ways.

But those naysayers grew bloated by eating crow, as Ohanti flew by theirs, and everyone else's, expectations.

Ohtani was motivated by his countryman, Ichiro Suzuki, as a child. Then Ohtani leaned on Ichiro's guidance when he struggled in his first spring training with the Angels, the one that saw him bat a not-so-robust .125.

Now, they are on the same level as the only two Japanese natives to win the MVP.

"Growing up I watched Ichiro and he won MVP, and it got me wanting to play in the big leagues someday," Ohtani said, through his translator, Ippei Mizuhara. "Hopefully, I can be that kind of figure to the kids watching me right now. And hopefully, even one day I could play with one of those kids that are watching me, which would be very special."

Ohtani's 2021 season was special indeed, the likes of which might never be seen again.

CHAPTER 16

OHTANI BRINGS HOME THE WBC TITLE THROUGH HIS WORDS AND ACTIONS

The World Baseball Classic had reached its final game, which had Shohei Ohtani digging into his soul. With Team USA standing between Team Japan and its third WBC title, the multi-talented Ohtani, at twenty-eight years of age, revealed yet another skill set and one that seldom arises.

Ohtani cleared his throat, and his teammates' eyes darted toward baseball's most recognized player in the center of Miami's loanDepot Park clubhouse. He quickly had their rapt attention, and now he sought their affirmation before the biggest nine innings of their lives.

"Let's stop admiring them," Ohtani said of the USA's major-league players possessing MVP and All-Star pedigrees. "If you admire them, you can't surpass them. We came here to surpass them, to reach the top. For one day, let's throw away our admiration for them and just think about winning."

That was certainly the mindset of Japan's citizens, as they hung on every WBC pitch, every hit, and every slice of the tournament's twists and turns while Japan attempted to prove its excellence in its nation's most important, and popular, sport.

They had packed the Tokyo Dome in the preliminary WBC rounds while clanging bells, chanting the Japanese players' names, and proving while there may be no crying in baseball, there is an opportunity for fun and showing national pride.

No one resides on a bigger pedestal to them than Ohtani, the sporting hero of their dreams and a person, according to one Japanese fan, with the weight of the country strapped across his massive shoulders.

"All the kids," the Japanese booster said, "want to be like Ohtani."

And why not?

Sure, the uncanny Ohtani had established himself against baseball's keenest competition by being named the American League Most Valuable Player in 2021 and the AL Rookie of the Year in 2018, thanks to his unconventional knack for elite pitching and hitting.

But to Japanese baseball enthusiasts, Ohtani's star had shone bright since the 2012 Summer Koshien, Japan's vaulted prep baseball tournament, while he was a seventeen-year-old student at Hanamaki Higashi High School. An Ohtani fastball reached a record 99 mph at that event, and soon his unlikely journey that led to his heartfelt pregame speech before the WBC final would be in full swing.

Ohtani played five years in Nippon Professional Baseball and was entering his fifth season with the Los Angeles Angels. The polite and gracious Ohtani was seemingly heaven-sent, and he had achieved a status among his compatriots that was unprecedented and unmatched, on or off the field.

The fifth WBC served as another showcase for Ohtani's greatness. Prior to the final against the USA, Ohtani had heaved the tournament's fastest pitch (102 mph), struck the hardest ball (118.7 mph), and smacked a homer (448 feet) that no one surpassed.

Ohtani was doing Ohtani things, which simultaneously were stunning and yet routine.

Mark DeRosa, the USA manager and a former major leaguer, joined everyone else in awe of Ohtani's attributes.

It's not that DeRosa, and others, hadn't seen a player dominate in countless ways on a diamond. The catch was that Ohtani was a gem at baseball's highest level.

"What he's doing in the game is what 90 percent of the guys in the clubhouse did in Little League or youth tournaments, and he's able to pull it off on the biggest stages," DeRosa said. "He is a unicorn to the sport."

Japan had sprinted to the final with a thrilling, walk-off victory over Mexico in the WBC semifinals. Before that pulsating victory, it claimed wins over squads from Italy, Australia, Czech Republic, South Korea, and China.

Meanwhile, USA, despite one misstep against Mexico, got past Cuba, Venezuela, Colombia, Canada, and Great Britain in advancing to the final.

The championship game matched not only the two best teams, but a pair of squads constructed to deliver a dramatic, game-ending script that will long be remembered.

"I was just thinking about all the people around the world watching the game," DeRosa said. "I was like, 'Wow, the baseball world's gonna win tonight regardless.'"

It was a tense battle prior to the epic showdown between Ohtani and Mike Trout, the three-time AL MVP and Ohtani's teammate with the Angels. It was Trout who was so instrumental in recruiting Ohtani to join the Angels for the 2018 season that Trout interrupted his wedding weekend to pitch Anaheim to Ohtani.

Now Ohtani was pitching to Trout, delivering triple-digit fastballs and a secondary pitch that was second to none.

"I think every baseball fan wanted to see that," said Trout, the USA captain. "I've been answering questions about it for the last month and a half. Did you think it was going to end in any other way?"

It was a seesaw affair leading to the monumental Ohtani-Trout at-bat.

Shortstop Trea Turner pushed USA ahead, 1-0, with his second-inning, WBC record-tying fifth home run of the event. Japan outfielder Munetaka Murakami, whose late homer in the semifinals helped eliminate Mexico, tied it with a second-inning, solo blast of his own.

Outfielder Lars Nootbaar, the first non-Japanese-born athlete to play for Japan, produced a bases-loaded, run-scoring groundout, also in the second, and when first baseman Kazuma Okamoto homered off lefty Kyle Freeland in the fourth, USA was staring at a 3–1 deficit.

USA's designated hitter Kyle Schwarber pulled his side to within 3–2 with an eighth-inning, 436-foot blast to center field off Yu Darvish, which led to Ohtani and Trout taking center stage in the ninth.

Ohtani had jogged to the bullpen twice to get loose, a somewhat tricky endeavor considering he was the designated hitter in Japan's lineup. But after Darvish, Ohtani's teenage idol, worked the eighth inning, the game was turned over to someone Darvish now looked up to—Ohtani.

Not only did Ohtani seek his first save since a 2016 playoff game while with the Nippon Professional Baseball Pacific League's Hokkaido Nippon-Ham Fighters, but he would have to navigate the part of USA's order that included the National League's reigning batting champion and three former MVPs.

What eventually followed was an indelible 15-pitch performance against some of the USA's best hitters that produced a carnival ride full of emotions.

Second baseman Jeff McNeil reached on a full-count walk when Ohtani didn't get a borderline pitch that clipped the bottom of the strike zone. Up next was right fielder Mookie Betts, who was among the WBC leaders with 10 hits. But after Betts quickly rolled into a 4-6-3 double play, Japan was one out shy of sending its nation into a frenzy.

Up strolled Trout as the two men who carried their respective nation's flags onto the field in the pregame introductions needed no introduction. Sharing space as Angels, they were now on opposite ends of the spectrum, with Trout trying to keep his team's fading hopes alive.

Trout, who had doubled earlier in the game, looked at his counterpart when entering the batter's box.

Ohtani didn't return the head nod, focusing instead on a strategy to retire the 10-time All-Star and a future first-ballot Hall of Famer.

"He's a competitor, man," Trout said. "That's why he is the best."

Ohtani's concentration was evident. So were the stakes.

"I was not expecting him to be literally the last batter of the game," Ohtani said. "I thought it was a possibility but I can't believe he was the last batter of the game."

The first pitch Trout saw wasn't a heater, but a slider that was shy of 90 mph. When Ohtani deciphered how well Trout tracked the ball and read it into the catcher Yuhei Nakamura's mitt, as if looking for something soft, Ohtani used that knowledge to his advantage.

Ohtani evened the count as Trout swung through an 100 mph fastball, which was center cut. Another 100 mph missile just missed outside, running the count to 2-1.

Another triple-digit fastball dissected the plate and it beat Trout again as his mighty swing came up empty.

Then Ohtani went with a low fastball that Nakamura couldn't handle, taking the count full and filling loanDepot Park with an electricity that stretched from the dugouts to the rafters.

Baseball's two grandest performers were delivering an incomparable slice of theater that underscored their greatness and grit. It all came down to one pitch, and the all-encompassing tension couldn't be ignored.

Ohtani had pumped in four straight fastballs and Trout had yet to make contact in flailing at two of them. The dramatic scene appeared to call for one more, with Ohtani wary of putting the tying run aboard by delivering something other than his best pitch.

Yet Ohtani, as he always has when it comes to baseball, looked at the situation through a different lens. With most of the sold-out crowd of 36,098 on their feet and expecting another fastball, Ohtani fooled them.

More importantly, he hoodwinked Trout.

With a sweeping slider that ran away from Trout, the sound that followed Ohtani's pitch was it hitting Nakamura's glove. Ohtani had won the enthralling battle by getting Trout to do something he seldom does: Swing and miss at three pitches in a single at-bat. In 6,174 career plate appearances in the majors, Trout had done so just 24 times.

With the ball safely and securely in Nakamura's possession, the celebration was on.

But first Ohtani had two more pitches, although instead of baseballs he flung his hat and glove with his prized right arm before being engulfed by his jubilant teammates.

"This is the best moment of my life," Ohtani would say.

A disappointed Trout wasn't distraught, but discouraged that he didn't deliver for his squad.

"It sucks that it didn't go the way I wanted it to," Trout said. "He won round one."

Japan had reached the top of the baseball world, with Ohtani proudly planting the nation's flag at the summit. Yet another dream for Ohtani had come true, with this one being accompanied by an entire country.

From Japan's prime minister to the ordinary Japanese citizens, Ohtani had delivered what they had all hoped for.

No title in a team sport comes exclusively from the production of one player, but Ohtani's heavy lifting in the WBC might be the exception.

Named the WBC's most valuable player, Ohtani batted .435 with a homer, four doubles, eight RBIs, and 10 walks. He also went 2–0 and notched a save while striking out 11 batters and pitching to a 1.86 ERA over 9 2/3 innings.

Cloud nine was where Ohtani, and anyone else associated with or cheering for Japan's title quest, landed after Trout fell short. His unproductive at-bat said more about Ohtani than it did about Trout.

Ohtani's final pitch not only finished off Trout, but it opened the debate regarding the talent gap between Ohtani and his peers.

"Great pitch," USA third baseman Nolan Arenado said. "If Mike Trout's not hitting it, I don't think anybody else is."

Of course, Ohtani is like nobody else, and that was among the biggest takeaways of his run through the WBC.

The WBC was a victory for all of baseball with a storybook ending that many had envisioned. But few realize just how much the title meant in the land of the rising sun.

"I thank you for giving tremendous courage and energy to all of Japan," said Fumio Kishida, Japan's prime minister, after meeting with the team. "Your huge achievement was possible because the power of each individual and the power of the team as a whole were combined, and I sincerely appreciated it."

The admiration for Ohtani, as well, only grows with no one really knowing its ceiling.

Thanks to Ohtani, Japan and its favorite son were now No. 1 in baseball's orbit. It seemed baseball revolved around Ohtani, instead of the other way around.